GLEN OF THE ROWAN TREES

On the Water of Unich

GLEN OF THE ROWAN TREES

TREES

And Other Stories

by

DUNCAN FRASER

MONTROSE:
STANDARD PRESS
1974

By the same author:

THE SMUGGLERS
HIGHLAND PERTHSHIRE
DISCOVERING EAST SCOTLAND

First published   -   -   -   -   1973
Second impression   -   -   -   1974

Printed at the Standard Press
Montrose, Scotland

The photographs of Glamis Castle are by Kenneth and June Hay, Montrose. Most of the others are by the author but he is indebted to the Keeper of the National Museum of Antiquities of Scotland for the Cairn Robie food vessel (p. 23), and to the National Library of Scotland for the three old maps (pp. 18, 24-25, 30). The Crown copyright photographs of Glamis Castle (p. 55), Edzell Castle (pp. 86, 87), the Crown Jewels (pp. 107, 113), Ardestie Souterrain (p. 131) and Claypotts Castle (p. 132) are reproduced by permission of the controller of H.M. Stationery Office.

CONTENTS

A souvenir of old Lochlee.

Glen of the Rowan Trees

What the girl was reading.

THERE IS something rather special about the rowan tree — the mountain ash. Certainly it is handsome, especially in the autumn, when it carries its great clusters of scarlet berries. But there is more to it than that. Of all the trees that grow in Britain, it has long been recognised as by far the most potent. An oak may look more virile, a silver birch more graceful and a copper beech more lovely against a background of greenery. But there is nothing supernatural about them. They would be no help at all if the witches were driving you frantic. When hell is all around, there is only one tree on which you can really depend. And that is the rowan.

So in olden times, when folk were closer to nature than now, almost every Scottish farmhouse, cottage and castle had a mountain ash growing somewhere close beside it. A benevolent spirit was said to live there, a guardian angel who protected the cattle and horses as well as the people.

In most places the rowans have largely disappeared. But in one Scottish glen, on the fringe of the Eastern Highlands, they still survive in their hundreds, in cottage gardens and at farmhouse doors. On lonely hillsides too you find them beside the ruins of many a but-and-ben. Glenesk is unusual that way. Even the road is

9

Lochlee, before it
became a reservoir
for North Angus

fringed in part with them. And mostly they are
very old. Few folk in the glen would willingly
cut down a rowan tree. They wait until it falls
down through sheer old age. And that, they
will tell you, is because it is such a pretty tree.

You may not realise at first how many there
are. The Rowan Hill is more immediately
obvious, for that is Glenesk's most familiar
landmark, a great dome of a hill with a monument on top and most of its long heathery
slopes bearing scarcely a tree of any kind. But
the ruins of old cottages can just be traced
round the foot of the hill and no doubt these
had their rowans when the peat fires were still
burning. The folk who lived there would have
told you that the power of the "ran-tree" was
no myth. Down in the Lowlands and up some
of the neighbouring glens, people without
rowans had to burn their witches. But no
roastings were needed in Glenesk. There is not
a scrap of evidence that any human being or
cattle beast ever came to harm as a result of
witchcraft there.

We shall be seeing the rowans again. But
first let us look around. High among the hills
rise the Lee and the Unich, two of the main
head-streams of the North Esk. They come
rippling through the heather, down towards the
ruined hamlet of Glenlee and the loch beyond,
and for many a century their moorland banks
were wolf country. The Unich has scarcely run
a mile from its source on the Lair of Aldararie,
when it is skirting round the base of a Wolf
Hill. Four miles to the north-west the Lee

comes cascading down from the heights, with a
Hunt Hill towering high on one side and a Wolf
Craig higher still on the other. In the same
parish, but in a less lonely part of it, one of the
last wolves in Scotland — perhaps the last of
them all — was hunted to its death scarcely
three centuries ago. And afterwards, for over
fifty years, people were afraid to believe that no
more were lurking around. The thought of being
attacked alive was not what worried them. But
to die among those hills and then meet the
wolves sent shivers down their spines.

In our time, the last of the wild goats too have
gone from those hills. Never very common, they
were always rather shy of human company and
not without cause. Men with guns tended to
think of sporrans as soon as they spied the rump
of a retreating wild goat. And yet alive they
were uncommonly handsome animals with their
great heads and their shaggy coats sweeping the
scree on the steep hillsides. Fully a quarter of
a century has passed since the last of them was
seen, in the lonely upper reaches of Glen Mark,
around Carlochy and beyond. Glen Mark was
their favourite haunt.

Some of the glensfolk too have been moving
away. Today Glenlee is so silent and deserted
that it is hard to think of a thriving hamlet
there. Yet it was once the largest clachan in
the glen and you can still see the ruins of old
cottages, where the Ennerdales at Dochty, the
Stewarts at Midtown, the Eggos at Little Brig
and others had their crofts until the middle of
last century.

10

There had been a time when, on Sunday mornings, nineteen bonneted men used to tramp down the glen and along the lochside, past the picturesque boathouse, to the church by the water's edge at the foot of the loch. But then Glenlee became part of a great deer forest, stretching as far as Glenisla in the west and Balmoral and the lands of the Marquis of Huntly in the north, and there was no longer room for all those crofters. After each funeral procession down to the church, it was only a matter of time until another cottage roof fell in. But the deer that took their place were worth seeing — great herds of three thousand around the bean-shed at the meeting of the waters in Glen Lee. Now those days too are gone, and so are the herds of even two thousand and one thousand. And still their numbers are dropping fast.

Lochlee had one eminent schoolmaster in Alexander Ross, who lived by the lochside for over half-a-century. He was the author of

Helenore, a narrative poem which Robert Burns described as "precious treasure", and it is still one of the great Scottish poems in the doric. But for us it has a special interest, for here we get our first glimpse of life in the upper glen two-and-a-half centuries ago. *Helenore* is the story of a girl who grew up there, until caterans came over the hills from Aberdeenshire, one day, and changed her whole life.

While Ross was writing, there were people around him who still remembered when witches used to be burned all over the civilised world. Scotland had fewer burnings than most countries but local folk had not forgotten the one at Milton of Clova, only eight miles across the hills.

And so, when he began his story with the birth of his heroine Nory, he described how the witches were kept at bay. There was a well tried ritual, known all over the country. With a red thread you tied two pieces of rowan wood together in the form of a cross and hung it over

The grave of Alexander Ross

11

the door. And that was a twofold protection, for everyone knew that —

> Ran-tree and red thread
> Gars the witches tak their speed.

It was not just that the witch had all her evil power drained out by the red thread. If anyone struck her with the cross, or even with a stick of rowan wood, the devil would carry her off to hell next time he came to claim his tribute. And though witches were rather proud of their meetings with him on social occasions in churchyards and elsewhere, they were strangely reluctant to join him in hell. They kept well away from houses that bore the rowan cross.

The cross had other uses too. Fixed to a cradle-head, it gave a child complete immunity during those most dangerous weeks between birth and baptism. If the risks at that time were becoming specially great, you could fasten a smaller rowan cross to the back of the infant's clothing for extra protection.

It was not just in Glenesk that the rowan was the great safeguard against witches. Several of those remedies were widely used throughout Britain and elsewhere in Europe. Even as late as the end of last century they were by no means forgotten on farms and in fishing villages along the Scottish coast. But in Glenesk, though the trees survived, those particular customs were gradually forgotten if they ever existed. Today, even among the oldest inhabitants it is widely believed that to have a tree beside the house was all that anyone needed. It was not so, however, when Alexander Ross was writing *Helenore,* upwards of two-and-a-half centuries ago. At the birth of his little heroine Nory, safeguards were used that may well have been peculiar to Glenesk. No cross was fastened above the door. But leaves were gathered from the rowan tree and scattered over the bed, just before the birth took place.

That was the first stage in a threefold ritual. A few hours later the folk gathered round in a circle to hear a solemn incantation intoned over the child's first nappie as it lay on the earthen floor. As a third and final stage, when her first vest was worn out a burning peat was taken from the fire and dropped through the garment. Not even the most wicked of witches could steal Nory from her mother and substitute a changeling after that.

Nory soon became the companion of a boy called Lindy who was two years older. He made daisy chains to hang round her neck. And not even a hen on a midden head guarded her

chicks from the greedy glaid more carefully than he guarded Nory. As she grew older she learned a favourite game of tig, in which the glaid — the kite — was the hunter. There were plenty of kites in those days. But now, like the wolf and the wild goat, they have vanished from the glen.

Before she was eight she was a shepherdess. Each morning, with Lindy, she took her father's sheep up to the grazing and there they would sit for hours on the hills, fashioning toys from rushes. Lindy was very much an expert. One day he wove a snood for her. Another time he twisted the rushes into one of those shell-shaped rattles called buckies, and put a stone inside to provide the rattle. Often the two children would be wearing rush hats of their own making, when they came back down the hill in the evening, with Helenore at the head of the flock and Lindy bringing up the rear.

It was not just because foxes and wild cats were more common than now that the sheep were brought down to the bughts each night. There were other reasons too. The ewes had to be milked. And in bad weather the sheep would have died like flies if they had been left on the hills. In more than half-a-century at Lochlee, Ross knew nothing about the Blackface and Cheviot breeds so common today. The old Highland sheep that he knew were small and delicate, some with white faces and some with pink. There was very little meat on them but they were not kept for eating. Their wool was long and beautifully soft.

As an eight-year-old, Nory had a considerable knowledge of first-aid and of herbs that were useful in an emergency. It was one of those skills that children were taught from their earliest days. And her knowledge was soon put to the test, when she found Lindy unconscious on the hillside, with blood pouring from a gash on his forehead. She stopped the bleeding with stench-grass and covered it over with a plantain leaf. You can still see plenty of stench-grass in the glen, though now its old name is forgotten and it is called yarrow instead.

Before Nory reached her teens she had stopped going to the herding and was helping her mother with the dairy work instead. By that time Lindy was no longer interested in rushes. He was spending hours building up his muscles with the putting-stane and practising his skill at the penny stane, a game rather like quoits that was played with flat round pebbles. But his interest in Nory was as strong as ever. One day, in a burst of old Presbyterian candour, he told

Loch Lee
from the old
schoolhouse.

his fourteen-year-old sweetheart:

> We maun marry now ere lang;
> Fouk will speak o's and fash us wi' the kirk
> Gin we be seen thegither in the mirk.

Perhaps it was not surprising that his thoughts were turning to marriage, for Nory was now an uncommonly pretty girl. The others looked like draff compared with her. In modern times she might well have won a title as Miss Glenesk, for she was as nimble as a roe-deer, as fresh as a trout, as supple as an eel. And probably you have noticed how coyly a flounder will bury itself in the sand if you stare too intently. She was like that — as modest as a fleuk.

But probably in the late summer even her sweet temper was sorely tried by the midges. Glenesk was once called "The Glen of the Midges" and when Ross was schoolmaster they seem to have been as plentiful as they are today, for he couldn't keep them out of his story. At one stage there were "clouds of midges reeling in the air". When Lindy recovered from an accident he was not merely well again but "as canty as a midge". And have you ever stopped to think how small a midge's wing must be? Alexander Ross had done that. When he was making the point that big troubles often grow out of very small beginnings, his phrase was: "Mischief frae a midge's wing may spring."

It was when Nory was fifteen that the caterans arrived. As a result of their visit, her father and Lindy finished up in a prison in the cateran leader's mansion. And she wandered some three miles into the hills and got lost. It was the first time she had been so far from home. There she met the Laird of Bonnyha', who was young and handsome and so wealthy that he ate beef whenever he felt inclined. And she fell so deep in love that she couldn't say no when he asked her: "Will you take a swinging laird as your husband?"

So there was a wedding at Lochlee. The laird brought the bridal gown, several bottles of wine and some ale for the feast — "An' O! the beer was pithy, brown and stout." But there was no whisky, which may seem odd in a glen where people still talk with awe about its old-time whisky-makers. It wasn't that Ross, as a respected schoolmaster and session clerk, was fastidious about mentioning whisky. Years later he wrote a sequel to *Helenore* and he had scarcely reached the fifteenth line when he was describing deliriously how whisky makes the heartstrings birl. The lack of whisky at the wedding was due to the simple fact that, when he was writing *Helenore*, the whisky-making had not yet begun. The sequel came years later, when the stills were in full production.

Two centuries have passed since Ross died but all trace of him has not yet vanished from Lochlee. A field's width north of the church you

The River Lee
just before it joins the Mark
to form the North Esk.

can still see where he had his combined schoolhouse and school. It was not a very pretentious building. At the schoolhouse end was a little window looking westward across the loch. And the loch was encircled by hills that blocked out the sun from his house for a month in midwinter. The east end was the schoolroom, more spacious than the part where he raised his large family, and yet scarcely ten feet square. A century ago enough of the roofless ruin remained for you to recognise the west window and the schoolroom fireplace at the other end, and the kailyard still had a fertile look. But now only the foundations are left.

There are more tangible remains in the nearby churchyard. The records tell us that in 1645 the church was destroyed by the army of the Marquis of Montrose. What we see now are the ruins of the one which was built soon after. Ross was its session clerk. It had a thatched roof until the year of his death and then the thatch was replaced with slates. But the church lasted for only a few more decades and then a new one was built elsewhere.

Alexander Ross and his wife, Jean Catanach, lie buried just inside the churchyard entrance in an honoured place at the gable-end of the church. At the foot of their grave is a monument which the glensfolk erected a century ago in memory of the old schoolmaster. It bears the inscription:

Above — The angel on the gravestone of Mrs Ross, who died in 1779.

Below — Crossed spades decorate the nearby grave of Al Brown, who died less than half-a-century earlier.

ERECTED
TO THE MEMORY
OF
ALEXANDER ROSS, A.M.,
SCHOOLMASTER OF LOCHLEE,
AUTHOR OF " LINDY AND NORY: OR
THE FORTUNATE SHEPHERDESS"
AND OTHER POEMS IN THE SCOTTISH DIALECT.
BORN APRIL 1699,
DIED, MAY 1784.
How finely Nature aye he paintit,
O' sense in rhyme he ne'er was stentit,
An' to the heart he always sent it
"Wi' might an' main";
An' no ae line he e'er inventit
Need ane offen'!

Beside the churchyard wall is another stone which Ross erected in memory of his wife, when he was living in his old age with his daughter at Buskhead. And it shows that he left his mark not only in literary circles but in this upland parish too. Even the art of stone carving saw changes during his years in the glen. The churchyard by the lochside has two examples of local gravestone carving, soon after his arrival. The angels on them, with heart-shaped heads, are

vastly different from the one which was carved on his wife's stone less than half a century later.

But it is time we moved on down the glen and scarcely a mile away is Invermark Castle. Four storeys high, with a small turret at its north-east corner, it stands on rising ground. It is a roofless ruin. Even its once considerable outbuildings vanished when the builders used it in 1803 as a quarry for a church and manse that were needed nearby.

But Invermark still deserves more than a passing glance. It was well placed, guarding the entrance to Glen Mark, one of the main hill passes between Angus and Upper Deeside. Herds of Highland black cattle grazed in Glen Mark in the summer and autumn of years long past and many a cateran band from Aberdeenshire crossed the mountains to round up the fattest of them. There are several stories of those wild reivers and the havoc they caused among the peaceful glensfolk.

They would, of course, have had little success if they had tried a frontal attack on the castle.

Even to reach the doorway they would have had to bring their ladders for it was some eight feet above ground level. And the door itself was guarded by an iron yett that came from elsewhere and was cut down to size. The yett is still in position and iron bars on several of the windows.

But perhaps we should not forget that, while Invermark guards one end of the pass, the Aberdonian lairds found it necessary to maintain an equally well defended castle at the other end. It is a sobering thought that there were black sheep in Angus as well as Aberdeenshire.

Probably Invermark Castle was built in 1526 and there in 1558 the death took place of the 9th Earl of Crawford, who bequeathed his soul "to the Omnipotent God and the whole Court of Heaven", and his body to be buried in his own aisle within the Church of Edzell.

The castle also formed the occasional residence of the Earl's son, Sir David Lindsay of Edzell, one of the most cultured men of his age. He built the unique walled garden at Edzell

Invermark Castle

16

The iron yett
at Invermark
Castle.

Castle and he also brought foreign miners to Glenesk.

It was about 1590 that Sir David decided to become a rich mine-owner. The minerals on his land were Crown property but he soon had them transferred to him. And the prospects were bright, for he had already found copper in two places, with a wealth of evidence that the metal existed in workable quantities. There were, of course, some minor difficulties. A Mr Lock, who had been granted the limestone rights, was none too pleased that no share of the other minerals was coming his way. He talked it over with Sir David, at Edzell Castle one day, and Sir David was left with a distinct impression that Mr Lock had spoken with "sic cholere as vas noch decent for ony man far les for a stranger". So Mr Lock had to go.

But the work went ahead. In a venture like this, with a fortune at stake, only the best was good enough and there was no doubt that the best mining engineers were Germans. A few years earlier one of them, Georgius Agricola, had produced the lavishly illustrated *De Re Metallica*, a magnificent textbook that covered the whole field. It was an outstanding example of Germany's long tradition of expert knowledge on mining in all its aspects.

Sir David decided to put a German in charge of his operations and by 1594 Bernard Fechtenburg had arrived in Glenesk to take charge of what seemed the most important part — the iron and copper working. Everyone agreed that this Bernard the Miner, as he called himself, was "very metal-like", with a thorough know-

ledge of every aspect of the subject. For fuel he was quite content to use peat instead of wood. But despite that, Sir David began to plant trees on a large scale to prevent any possible shortage of fuel.

There was only one small problem. Sir David's special interest in mining was prompted partly by financial troubles. He was deep in debt and apt to forget about paying wages. His brother Lord Menmuir was quick to realise the danger involved. Their German miner, like most good craftsmen, was temperamental and liable to go elsewhere unless he was regularly paid his £3 12s per week. So he suggested that Fechtenburg's wages should be paid by Sir David's carline, who had a better memory than her husband. Finding a furnished house with a kailyard, for Herr Fechtenburg and his wife, was also left to her. And Lady Lindsay went further than that. From the cloth she wove at the castle she gave the man enough for a coat, a cloak and a pair of breeks.

So, with everything happily settled, the mining began. Soon a smelting house for iron was erected near the foot of the glen, across the river from Dalbog, and local folk learned the

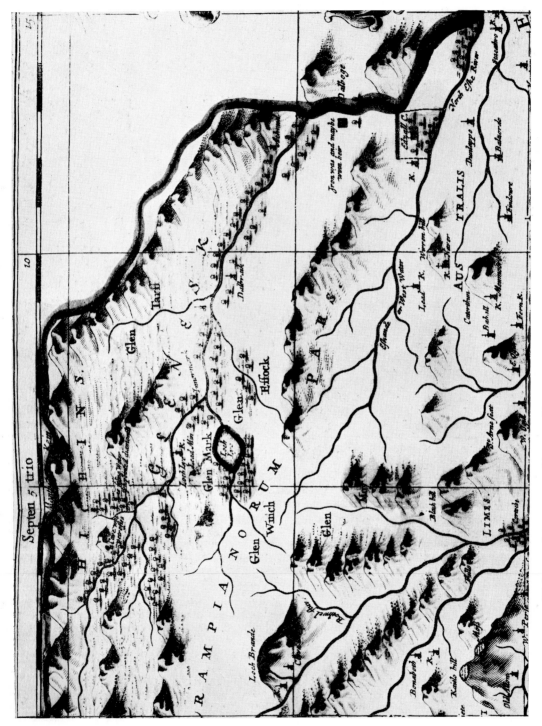

Eighteen miners were working at Gilfumman when the Rev. Robert Edward drew this map in 1678.

18

skills of the trade, for Bernard the Miner used local labour. How well and how long his iron-works prospered in the Wood of Dalbog is now unknown. It ceased before the Rev. Robert Edward made his map of Angus in 1678, for it merely records of Dalbog that "iron was and may be winn heir".

In 1602 Sir David brought another German expert, Hans Ziegler of Nuremberg. The iron-working must still have been continuing then, for it was expressly excluded from Herr Ziegler's contract, which included only gold, silver, quicksilver, copper, tin and lead. But there was every indication that the new contract was going to develop into a major enterprise. Ziegler was granted authority not only to search for metals but "to big and erect towns and burghs beside the same mines, to create baillies, officiars and other members within the samyn, to hald courts and to do justice thereintil . . . for the space of twenty-five years."

It was around Invermark Castle that those metals were most likely to be found and the towns and burghs erected. Only a stone's throw beyond the castle, on the way to Loch Lee, a hollow on the right-hand side of the road was being pointed out a century ago as a former gold-mine. And the story goes that, three miles from there, the River Tarf contained so much that a lucky lad at Gracie's Linn was able to fill his pockets with it. A disused quarry at Dal-brack, across the river from the Rowan Hill, was also being pointed out as a copper mine. And certainly there was copper ore in that district, for a boy found a sample of it between Dalbrack and Glen Effock, only about twelve years ago. The main discoveries in that part of the glen, however, were lead and silver.

About sixty years after Sir David Lindsay's death, the biggest of the lead mines was dis-covered by his great-grandson about a mile and a half up Glen Mark from Invermark Castle. It was above Cowiehillock plantation on the steep east end of Gilfumman; but there was no plantation on Cowiehillock in those days. In 1678 the mine was in full production, with eighteen miners digging deeper every day, and by that time they had reached a large vein of ore which yielded a 54th part of silver when properly refined. The vein was thought to be inexhaustible. Within a few years, however, the mine became flooded and, though there was no insurmountable difficulty about drawing off the water, the work was abandoned.

In 1728 the miners returned to Gilfumman to make a survey for the South Sea Company but they had to report there was not enough lead to make mining worthwhile. Another century passed and then a souvenir of that survey was unearthed. In 1845 the Glenesk correspondent of the "Montrose Standard" sent a news paragraph to his editor: "We have seen a shilling of the South Sea Company, found upon the parsonage at Tarfside by the Rev. Alex. Simson's servant David Low. He refuses to sell it, as being a specimen of the Lochlee silver." The corres-pondent added that, though local folk had made several attempts to smelt ore from the Glenesk mines, all they had succeeded in extracting was "a dull substance something like lead".

There has been no further mining at Gil-fumman but even from the road the workings can still be seen on the hillside. Water from the entrance trickles down the steep slope to disappear in the plantation below and carbon is clearly visible in the gravel along its route. But no fortunes came to the Lindsay family out of this mining. Financial worries dogged them all their days.

Upper Glenesk revives memories of other things besides mining. In 1746, after the battle of Culloden a prominent Jacobite fugitive, the laird of Balnamoon, hid for many months in a cave in the lonely upper reaches of Glen Mark, with only the wild goats for company. Still known as Balnamoon's Cave, it is about a mile and a half beyond the Queen's Well and is reached by crossing the river and continuing upstream by a track between Carlochy and the river. The track disappears in a wide stretch of firm ground but reappears later. The cave, about 75 feet above the river bank, is not easy to see, as the ground above and around is very rocky. It has a grassy top and built-up stones on each side, with a narrow vertical slit as an entrance.

There was a large price on Balnamoon's head but, though his hiding place was known to many in the glen, it was never revealed to the troopers or the spies who were searching for him. One rainy night, however, he was very nearly caught. Dressed as a servant he was sitting by the kitchen fire in a farmhouse in Glen Mark, when suddenly into the kitchen came a party of soldiers in search of him. The farmer swore on his solemn oath he had not seen him for weeks. Then, offering the visitors a meal to warm them, he gruffly ordered Balna-moon out to clean the byre. While the soldiers settled round the fireside, the fugitive lost no time in getting back across the muir to his cave.

Eventually he was allowed to return to his estate and for the rest of his life he never forgot the debt he owed to this farmer of Glen Mark, who was always a welcome guest at his home near Brechin.

*Queen
Victoria
on
Lochnagar.*

Queen Victoria knew Glen Mark. She passed that way more than once on visits from Deeside to Glenesk and on those occasions she made the acquaintance of one of the celebrities of the glen, Jeems Mitchell, a tall brawny Highlander who eventually became a head keeper in the glen, like his son and his grandson after him. There is a delightful though slightly apocryphal story that on one occasion, when he was leading the Queen's pony from the shoulder of Mount Keen down by the Ladder Burn to Glen Mark, it stumbled and shied on the steep descent. And with a shrewd knowledge born of long experience he told Her Majesty: "That's a damned fitterin' brute o' a powney o' yours, Mistress Queen."

The best remembered of those royal visits to Glenesk was in September 1861. With Prince Albert and several members of her Court, the Queen had lunch with Lord Dalhousie in Glenmark Cottage at the foot of the Ladder Burn. She drank from a spring in the middle of the valley about three hundred yards farther on, and then they continued their journey to Fettercairn, where in the guise of a marriage party from Aberdeen they spent the night in the homely little village inn. For Queen Victoria that journey was among the last of her carefree memories. Within a few weeks her husband, the Prince Consort, was dead.

A stone arch, flanked by battlemented towers, was built in Fettercairn to commemorate this royal visit and in the wilds of Glen Mark another memorial was raised by Lord Dalhousie — an imperial crown, nearly twenty feet high, surmounted by a cross, over the spring from which the Queen had drunk. There is a width of ten feet between each of the six flying buttresses of granite, and beneath them the water flows into a basin inscribed —

> Rest, traveller, on this lonely green,
> And drink and pray for SCOTLAND'S QUEEN.

On one of the buttresses a black marble slab bears the inscription —

> Her Majesty, QUEEN VICTORIA,
> and his Royal Highness the PRINCE CONSORT
> visited this Well and drank of its refreshing
> waters,
> on the 20th September, 1861,
> the year of Her Majesty's great sorrow.

* * *

Now we are beyond the Mark and on our way down the glen. Opposite a large spruce tree we pass what is left of the old inn at Cross-style. Inns were plentiful once. There was another behind the manse in Rotten Haugh, at the entrance to Glen Mark, and there until the middle of last century you could still buy a glass of home-brewed beer.

From here the road to Tarfside is a modern one which did not exist in bygone times. The old one, more direct and more hilly, branches off towards Westbank and the north side of the Rowan Hill. As we reach the end of this old road the smell of whisky is growing strong and

20

The Queen's Well.

tales of brave men and bloody fights come dirling through our heads.

But let us forget about the whisky for a moment and think instead of King Robert the Bruce. It is said that in the winter of 1306, before his throne was yet secure, he fought a battle here to subdue the powerful Red Comyn, Earl of Buchan. Dozens of artificial cairns round the foot of the Rowan have long been regarded as the burial mounds of those who died in that battle. By the side of the old glen road, about a mile due west of Tarfside, is a stone with a carving of a cross. Here the King is said to have planted his Royal Standard before the battle began. And several miles farther down the glen, beside the fence on the right-hand side, at a bend in the road immediately before you reach the Retreat, the stone can be seen where Bruce is reputed to have sharpened his sword after that bloody engagement. As one looks at the stone with its deep criss-cross grooves, one shudders to think what a shocking mess the King must have made of his sword in the sharpening!

Historians, unfortunately, are not too enthusiastic about any part of this legend. They point out that, though Bruce was in fact in the district, he was so ill that he had to be carried on a litter for months and he was avoiding battles at all costs. Though no one is entirely sure when

and why the cairns were built at the Rowan, it was almost certainly not in connection with any battle. Some think they are prehistoric mounds. Others will tell you they were gathered in very much later times to provide better grazing for the cattle on this stretch of commonty.

On one point, however, we can be sure — that not every cairn in Glenesk is just a heap of uninteresting stones. Some odd things can happen, when you look into them. You might even see a wild cat glaring out at you with baleful eyes. And you don't need to go to the remotest parts of the glen for that. One winter's day, some years ago, a gamekeeper was sitting by his fireside at civilised Millden, when he had a curious feeling that he was being watched. He turned round very quickly and there, looking in at the window with its paws on the sill and its nose against the glass, was a wild cat. For an instant their eyes met and then it was gone. Moments later he too was out of the house in hot pursuit. And the tracks were easy to follow on the snow-covered ground, up the Turret Burn and over the Modlach, and down past Dalhastnie, to a cairn on the river bank opposite Greenburn Farm. There they stopped. He went home for a dog ferret to flush out his prey, and he shot it beside the cairn.

But it was not a wild cat that nine-year-old Mary Birse saw in another cairn, over a hundred

Mystery cairns beside the Whisky Road.

years ago. There is an ancient road that comes from the Lowlands up Glen Lethnot and over the Clash of Wirran into Glenesk, then on by Deeside to Moray and Nairn. In earlier times, long strings of ponies crossed the hills by that road with whisky for the thirsty Lowlanders. And though the traffic had ceased before Mary was born, she knew it as the Whisky Road. It crossed the North Esk at Dalbrack, rounded the west side of the Rowan Hill and, after passing Stylemou', climbed the shoulder of Cairn Robie before plunging downhill into Arsallary. Mary knew that part of the road very well indeed.

And so, when she took her dog for a walk one day in 1861, they went up the Whisky Road. They reached the crest on Cairn Robie and then a sudden rustle in the heather sent the dog chasing after a rabbit. Both disappeared into a large mound of stones by the roadside. Mary got down on her hands and knees and peered in to see what was happening. And that was how she discovered that inside the cairn was a stone box, about four feet long and roughly made of slabs, with a large slab for a lid. The dog and the rabbit were inside the box. They had company, too, for lying quietly beside them was a skeleton with its knees drawn up to its chin. And, in spite of all the commotion, an earthenware pot beside the skeleton was still unbroken. Crudely scratched with a distinctive design, it was about $5\frac{1}{2}''$ in height.

The cist
in the cairn
on Cairn Robie.

The skeleton didn't alarm the girl. People aren't afraid of skeletons in Glenesk. But her parents were terrified when she arrived home and told them what had happened, for no tenant's dog was allowed to kill rabbits in those days. They remembered how the folk at Shanna, near the foot of the glen, had been evicted when they were caught with one of the laird's rabbits. People still talked about their last act of defiance. With all the family possessions loaded on a cart, they set the but-and-ben ablaze before leaving. But probably that didn't worry the laird unduly. Rabbits were more important. They were scarce and very precious.

The Birses kept their grim secret. Not a whisper about their dog's crime ever reached the laird. But after the skeleton had slept

The bowl
that Mary Birse saw.

on for a few more months, the same thing happened again. This time a keeper's terrier was the culprit and when the rabbit's squeals had died away it was the dog's turn to howl, for it couldn't get out. When the keeper was rescuing it he discovered the cist, and since he had no need to be silent the cairn was opened up. The earthenware pot was sent to Edinburgh, to the National Museum of Antiquities where it can be seen to this day. And high on the Whisky Road, just beside a fence on the brow of the hill, you can still see the cist in its cairn, a few yards from the roadside. Its last inhabitant was not the skeleton. Many years after its discovery, Mary Birse's son Jim was caught in a blizzard on the hill. For half-an-hour he sheltered in his mother's cist. And he was able to report to her on his arrival home that it was "fine and comfortable".

But it was not in the days of King Robert the Bruce that the old man on Cairn Robie was buried beneath his cairn with his food vessel and his knees tucked up. That happened in the early Bronze Age, some three thousand five hundred years ago. It was not the only Bronze Age relic found in the glen.

As for the Cross Stone, though Bruce almost certainly never planted his standard there, it must have been familiar to the glensfolk for centuries before he was born. The cross, with its deep-cut circles where the lines intersect, is a crude but genuine example of Pictish workmanship, carved almost certainly by a pupil of St Drostan — for the Saint lived in this lovely glen for many years around 600 A.D. His name

23

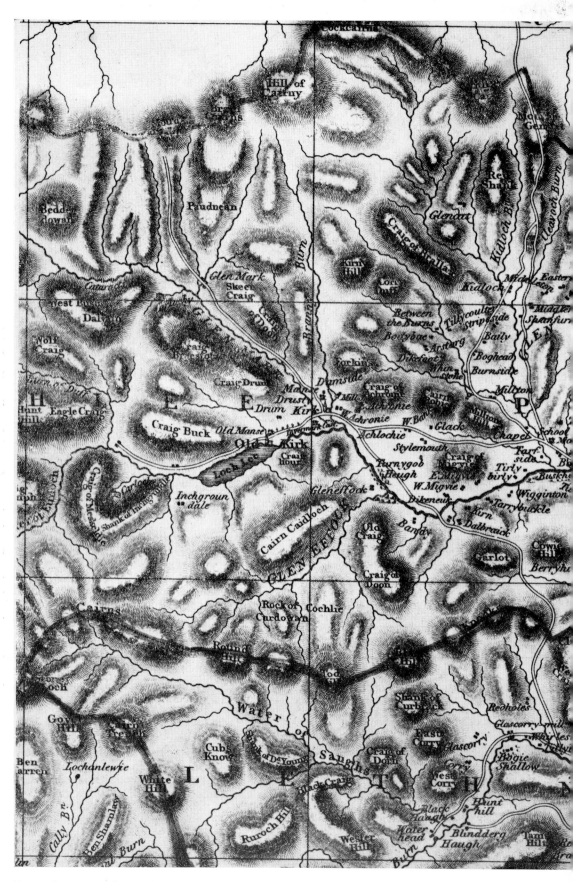

From Thomson's Atlas 1825

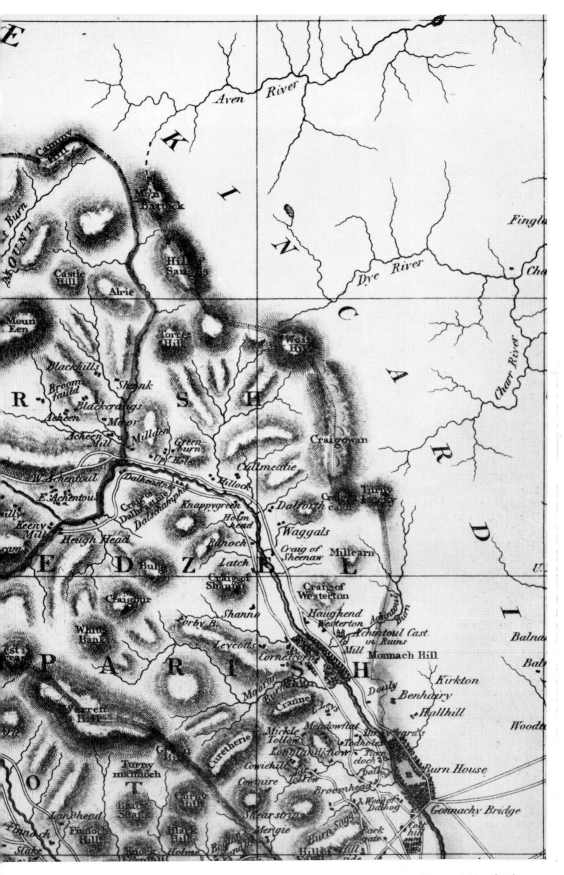

Glens of North Angus

The Cross Stone

still lingers on. The House of Mark, formerly the manse of Lochlee, was commonly called Droustie and a fountain nearby is Droustie's Well. A stretch of ground near the Parsonage at Tarfside used to be Droustie's Meadow and at the foot of the glen, at Neudos, is another St Drostan's Well. Even the old church at Loch Lee was sometimes called the kirk of Droustie. It is recorded that, when the saint died in Glenesk, his remains were carried across the hills in state and buried in a stone coffin in the Aberdeenshire churchyard at Aberdour.

According to tradition, the Cross Stone used to be farther up the glen and was not moved to its present position until early last century. It is perhaps worth noting that the old name of Westbank is Auchlochrie, which means "The Field of the Stone". And that part of the glen was not only an early religious centre. Towards the end of the eighteenth century it was also one of the growth points in a local industry almost but not quite as spiritual. The glensfolk were starting to make whisky.

Whisky-making, at that time, was an almost essential sideline in all the Angus glens — the one sure safeguard to stop the drift to the cities. It provided the crofters with all the financial advantages of city life and none of its disadvantages. And because the Glenesk crofters were sober and practical folk, they did very well from their whisky, which tasted far better than the Lowland trash that was then on sale. There was no depopulation in Glenesk, all the time its whisky-making lasted. Over

26

the hills in Glenisla there was none either. But when the stills were closed Glenisla lost almost half its inhabitants.

During the forty years of the whisky-making there were stills on the hill burns of nearly all the Angus glens but these together were far from enough to meet the urgent Lowland demand. Much larger supplies were needed and these came from away to the north — from Deeside and more distant Morayshire along the well-trod Whisky Road. With scouts ahead and on either side, keeping watch for the excisemen, the long strings of pack ponies came over the hills by moonlight, and by break of day their loads had vanished from sight.

No hiding place at a time like that was more popular and respected than the manse of some friendly parson. A minister at Fern, on the Lowland fringe, was often a veritable godsend. And so too was the Rev. Peter Jolly, parson for many years of the Episcopal churches of Glenesk and Lethnot. His parsonage at Stylemou' was actually on the Whisky Road, close to where it crossed the old road down Glenesk. You can still see its ruins. It was almost within sniffing distance of the whisky still on the Rowan Hill and those who had something to hide were always sure of a brotherly welcome at his friendly home. All through the day the cargoes would lie hidden and as night fell they would be reloaded. With extra supplies from Glen Effock, Inchgrundle, Craig Soales and the Rowan, the procession would head south again on its final stage — across the river at Dalbrack, up the Cowie Hill, over the high moorland and down the Clash of Wirran into Lethnot, then on to the Lowlands.

All trace of those old whisky days has not yet vanished from the glen. High up Glen Effock, astride the stream, the ruins of one whisky bothy can still be seen. Most of its out-put is said to have gone to Forfar. The Free-masons of Lochlee, in their old lodge at Dykeneuk, could get an ample supply too within easy reach, for on the burn that came from the Rowan Hill down past their lodge room was another whisky bothy. Its ruins look uncomfort-ably close to the public road today. But then it was better hidden from prying eyes, for the road had not yet been moved from the other side of the hill.

A mile and a half farther down the glen, the

*The old parsonage at Stylemou'
with Westbank beyond.*

*The
Whisky Bothy
on the Rowan.*

villagers of Tarfside were in whisky country too. Some of the water they drank was used to condense the vapour in the Townhead still before it reached Tarfside. And three miles to the north you could distil your liquor in more remote surroundings by the burnside in Glen Cat.

But it is unlikely that any of these had an output to compare with yet another still, high on a hillside above Glenlee. It was a long trudge up the hill to this one, with the mash on your back. But, with nineteen bonneted men in the hamlet down below, there was no shortage of labour. And though the excisemen were more than a little suspicious, they could see nothing — either from the hamlet itself or from across the loch at Inchgrundle. Perhaps, if they had noticed a tall black rock half-a-mile north of the top of Loch Lee and had gone half-a-mile westward from there, they would have been more successful. With its outbuildings it was tucked out of sight in a hollow between Craig Buck and Craig Terran. And probably there

were several other stills too that are now forgotten.

Only six years ago a souvenir of those days came to light during a grouse drive on Craig Soales, when a gamekeeper's foot struck a metal object half buried in the ground. He marked the spot with two white stones and when the day's beating was over he returned to collect his find. It was curiously shaped, with three projecting pipes.

The gamekeeper recognised it as the head of a still and it went into the Glenesk Folk Museum. You could have guessed it came from an illicit still, for there had never been a licensed one within twenty miles, while on a hill burn only half-a-mile away you can still find a ruined whisky bothy. The three pipes, however, were the surest proof. In all the records of whisky-making, legal and illegal, there seems to be no evidence that still heads were ever made with more than a single pipe, until this one was found in Glenesk. It may have been a local invention. But though the three pipes were

Arsallary

from beside the burial cairn of the Bronze Age folk,
on the Whisky Road.

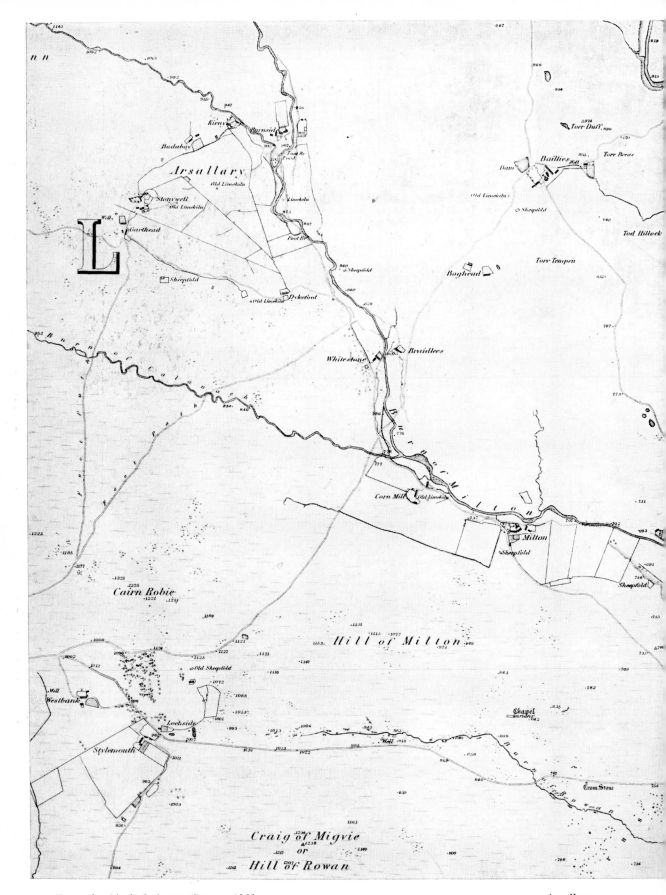

From the 6-inch Ordnance Survey, 1865

Arsallary

The limekiln at Migvie.

maybe unique, there was no doubt about their purpose. For anyone wanting to make whisky in a hurry, a still head with three pipes had very real advantages.

And now let us return from the bothies to the Whisky Road and follow the route that Mary Birse took with her dog, that day she found the skeleton. We carry on, past the cairn with its cist and down the other side of Cairn Robie into the secluded wonderland beyond, where you have the sheep and the grouse for company. Peat smoke used to rise from the chimneys of White Stone and Kirny, Atween Ye Burns, Breedless, Garthhead and Turnymuck. Now they are all in ruins. This was once the thriving hamlet of Arsallary, and here at Burnside in bygone days they used to keep the peat fire burning day and night — for two hundred and fifty years, until the 1930s — to prevent ill luck befalling them. And the odd thing is that near the foot of the glen was another house where they carefully put the fire out each night for the same sensible reason.

Arsallary had other things besides fires that burned day and night. Its souvenirs of the whisky days are all around. Finding enough grain for the distillers had not been easy at first. Though there was always enough barley in the parish to meet the needs of the glensfolk, there wasn't enough for whisky too, until the rich landowners along the coast let them into a

secret. They could get bigger crops — they might even be able to reclaim part of their moorland — if they sweetened the land with liberal doses of lime. There was limestone all around. And, just about the time when the whisky-making began, limekilns began to appear like mushrooms at almost every cottage door up and down the glen.

Arsallary had more than its share of them. In this little corner, off the beaten track, there were six within a radius of about half-a-mile — at Stonywell, Badalair, Burnside, Dykefoot, Milton and the Baillies. The whisky-making stopped about 1829 and the use of the kilns stopped too. Only one of them — the one at Burnside — was still producing lime when engineers made a survey for the 6-inch Ordnance Survey map published in 1865. Each of the others is shown on the map as an "old limekiln". There wasn't any point in going to so much trouble in liming the land, if you weren't making whisky. And the limestone anyway wasn't very good. It was much too sandy.

But in Arsallary the end of the whisky trade brought ruin not just to the kilns. Without the whisky there was no longer a livelihood for anyone. And so the folk packed their belongings and moved elsewhere. The whole hamlet was gradually engulfed in ruins. It happened more than a century ago but you can still see the tumbledown cottages — the most impressive of

31

*The malt kiln,
Whigginton.*

all the memorials to Glenesk's lost craft of whisky-making.

Even to this day the Burnside kiln is still one of the best preserved in the whole of Glenesk. Among other good examples are those at Migvie, Corhairncross and Whigginton. Corhairncross was probably the last place in the glen where distilling went on and it was here, beside the bridge over the river, that the last water-kelpie was seen in the glen. Corhairney was on his way home from a masonic function when he saw it. And talking about Corhairney reminds us that even to this day the local folk haven't quite got accustomed to the use of surnames. People are known instead by the name of their house. So Alex Stewart of Buskhead was always Eck Buskie and Nanny Davidson at Stylemouth was Nanny Stylem. And even when Dunbar of Garthhead moved to Drumgreen, the old name of Garthie stuck to him. But we are forgetting about the kilns.

Though Whigginton had no water kelpie, it had in addition to its limekiln another much rarer kind of kiln. And it had a notable inhabitant too in Jess Cattanach, the glen's last kinswoman of Alexander Ross, the poet. A commanding figure, almost six feet tall, she spent almost all her life at Whigginton and she was within four years of being a centenarian when she died there in 1919. Yet almost certainly not even Jess had any idea what the purpose was of her egg-shaped kiln. Her neighbour, Mrs Stewart of Buskhead, was within days of being a centenarian when she died recently, and certainly she never discovered

Jess Cattanach was in her late nineties when she
died at Whigginton in 1919.

what it was, though she knew it was there. It
was only recently recognised as a corn or malt
kiln, one which could have been used either for
drying the grain crop or for taking it along the
first stage on the road to becoming whisky.
Crofters' malt kilns had gone out of use by 1794,
long before the limekilns. They were probably
never entirely successful, for they tended to
catch fire and burn the grain. But they too are
almost certainly among the souvenirs of the
whisky days.

There are other souvenirs too of those days,
though not of the whisky. In a glen where
people were mostly vegetarian and dairy herds
were large, cheese was a vital part of the daily
diet. There are several cheese presses, upwards
of two centuries old, in the glen — at The
Retreat, Migvie, Dalforth and elsewhere.

Arsallary is now swallowed up in one large
sheep farm. They are Blackface sheep and like
dogs and salmon they seem to have a homing
instinct. The lambs are taken down to the Lowlands for the winter and when they are brought
up next year you could release them all at one

central spot if you cared. They would sort
themselves out and return by instinct to the
hillsides they knew before. Other breeds would
get sadly lost if you tried to do that with them.

You are in a district now where there are
some well known hill paths. Shinfur, where
the Tarf and the Tennet meet, is the start of
an ancient road to the north. It forks at the
Kedloch, the path to the left being the Fir
Mount road, reputed to be the oldest hill path
in Scotland, while the one to the right is the
Birse Mount road which crosses northward by
the Sloch.

And now let us go down through Arsallary
to the bridge over the Tarf at Tarfside. Here we
can join the main glen road or we can turn
right, on to the rough track which climbs steep
up to the higher moorland. This is the old glen
road which runs between the Rowan and the
Milton Hill, and then by Westbank towards
Invermark.

On this road, on your left, is the Pictish Cross
Stone and north-west of it, on the hillside, are
the foundations of the old Episcopal church

c

*Glenesk
Folk
Museum*

where the Rev. Peter Jolly used to lead his whisky-makers in their devotions. The glen folk worshipped there for close on two centuries and were overwhelmingly Episcopalian. At one time the little church is said to have had a congregation of 600, some of whom travelled from as far as the Forest of Birse, across the mountains in Aberdeenshire.

The first parson of this church on the Milton Hill was the Rev. David Rose. He had a Presbyterian rival in the Rev. John Scott, who lived in Invermark Castle and preached in the church at Loch Lee. And Mr Scott was none too pleased when he heard that at one service in the chapel, in 1745, no less than seventy new members were confirmed. Everyone knew, of course, that the chapel folk were a pack of Jacobites. So, as a loyal British subject, Mr Scott had Mr Rose arrested within days of the start of the Jacobite Rising later that year.

After Culloden, when the Argyll Highlanders were scouring the glen for Jacobite fugitives like Balnamoon, they destroyed this chapel so thoroughly that scarcely a stone was left unturned. It was still a ruin two years later, when Mr Scott came riding down the road on his way to a Presbytery meeting in Brechin. Almost exactly opposite the chapel he was thrown from his horse and killed. And that was a judgment upon him.

The chapel's congregation had to wait until 1763 before they dared build themselves a new place of worship. When they did make a start it took a week to build and with its thatched roof it lasted for fifty years.

Mr Jolly spent his latter days in Tarfside and now we retrace our steps in that direction too. There are trout to watch, from the bridge over the Tarf, and Tarfside beyond is the only village in the glen. Its Masonic Hall is the hub of life in the parish. Here the concerts and dances are held, and when there is a dance at Tarfside everyone is there — young children and great-grandmothers and teenagers alike.

The road leads on down the glen to the Birks of Ardoch and here among the trees is the Retreat, once a shooting lodge and now a folk museum and tearoom, with a handicrafts shop attached. It is in many ways a remarkable place. No other glen in Scotland has a folk museum of its own and many a county might be envious of this one. In large part it was created by a native of the glen, Miss Greta Michie, who has combed its every corner to build up a unique collection of old historical documents and relics of bygone days. But it has grown into more than that. Everyone has become involved, in a wide variety of ways.

The museum is a lively place. As you walk around, rubbing shoulders with the past, you hear snatches of authentic glen music and even the reminiscences of old inhabitants, tape-recorded. Altogether it creates an impressive picture of how the glensfolk lived in bygone

Cheese Press
at Glenesk Folk Museum.

Meal time at the Retreat

days when work was hard and money scarce and the quality of life was rich. Not least impressive are the many relics of old farming methods and craft industries — the ploughs, the flechter-spades, the country blacksmith's forge.

All around, among the Birks of Ardoch, you can see the rowan trees laden with berries in autumn time. Yet oddly enough in the farming room there is no sign of rowan wood, though elsewhere — all over Britain — it was regarded as almost essential. Cattle beasts were so often the target of the witches that no laddie would have dreamt of cutting a stick from any other tree when he went to the herding. That would have been inviting the cows to go mysteriously dry. In the dairy too, a pin of rowan wood in the churn would banish all risk in the butter-making. In fact, there was scarcely a farming implement that wasn't better to have at least one small part made of rowan wood. But in the farming room at the Glenesk museum you will search in vain for these. There is not even a rowan cross from above some old barn door — or the memory of such a cross, though memories are long in the glen. The Davidsons of Migvie have had joiners in their family for well over a century and a half, but even they have not heard of those old customs. It almost seems true, as they say in the glen, that if you grew enough of the bonny rowan trees you would need no further protection.

The Retreat is one of the special attractions of Glenesk. High on the moorland behind the museum is another — the silver mine on Craig Soales. But don't expect to find too much silver. Though the Craig Soales mine is better recorded than the one at Gilfumman, it has always produced more discussion than silver.

To reach it, you go up the glen beyond the Retreat to the first gate in the fence on your right and there a path leads through the Birks of Ardoch, skirting to the left of some ruined cottages, to the edge of the moorland beyond. Then you make for an isolated tree, over on the

"You will bring out a handful of slag"

*Round
holes
on the
hillside.*

left, and from it a fence can be seen stretching up the hillside. You head for a gate in this fence, at right-angles to the fence and well up the hill slope.

On the way, you pass the ruins of a hamlet and close on your right are traces of run-rig cultivation, with the ridges clearly marked between the furrows. These take you back almost a century and a half. And so you reach the fence gate. Only a short distance beyond is the end of the hollow containing the Craig Soales mine. It had vastly more lead than silver, but neither in any great quantity. The early eighteenth century was its heyday, when the York Buildings Company tried without success to exploit its mineral wealth.

The rock face where they quarried can still be seen and there are some mysteries round about. The bed of the valley in front of the face and the moorland ridge above are pitted with round holes, about four feet deep and some well over six feet in diameter. In summer, like great bowls brimming over with bracken, they contrast oddly with the surrounding heather. There are about fifteen of them, mostly on the edge of the ridge above the mine. And no one can say with certainty what their purpose was, though almost certainly they were used for the smelting.

Some two centuries earlier, Georgius Agricola described in his *De Re Metallica* how smelting might be done in such hollows. "In Westphalia," he wrote, "they heap up ten wagon-loads of charcoal on some hillside which adjoins a level place, and the top of the heap being made flat, straw is thrown upon it to the thickness of 3 or 4 digits. On the top of this is laid as much pure

lead as the heap can bear; then the charcoal is kindled, and when the wind blows it fans the fire so that the ore is smelted. In this wise the lead, trickling down from the heap, flows on to the level and forms broad thin slabs."

Though that may solve the mystery of the hollows, another still remains. The mine is in a little valley, the slopes of which rise steep on each side to the moorland above. Most of the hollows are on top of one of those slopes. There are no hollows on top of the other slope. Yet here, if you dig your fist into the turf, you will bring out a handful of slag. This is the only place where the slag has been found. And it seems somewhat odd that anyone should laboriously carry it from the hollows down the slope, across the valley and up the other side, to dump it on top of the opposite ridge. On that subject Agricola provides no clues.

A little farther down, the old road used to cross the Modlach at a much higher level than now, and there were fatal accidents in the winter snowstorms. Early in the 19th century the Freemasons of the glen built a tower by the roadside to serve as a refuge for those who were caught in a sudden storm. Out of sight of the modern road, the tower still stands beside the old track, with an inscription above the doorway: "St Andrew's Tower, built 1826." The door has disappeared but you can still see the masonic emblems above the tower and the three projecting stones inside which served as seats.

One tragedy on that old hill track is still not forgotten. We have already met the Rev. Peter Jolly at his parsonage on the Whisky Road. In 1811 he moved to a new one at Tarfside and

The Craig Soales Mine

St Andrew's Tower.

just about the time when the tower was built he attended a wedding at the other side of the Modlach at the Mill of Aucheen. A Miss Douglas, who had been one of the guests, was travelling back over the old road with him, when they were caught in a storm and lost all sense of direction. Early next morning she died in his arms and the minister himself was more dead than alive when a search party reached him.

The new road lower down the hill has not solved all the old problems. There are still wintry blizzards when it too is blocked. And so, near the crest of the road, two snowploughs lie in readiness all the year round.

At Millden, the shooting lodge at the foot of the Modlach, we move out of Lochlee parish into the neighbouring one of Edzell. The Burn of Turret, coming down from Mount Battock, forms the dividing line. And we are leaving

behind us too what has aptly been called "the glen of glens", for Lochlee parish contains an abundance of them — Glenlee and Glen Mark; Glen Effock; Glencat and Glentennet, two branches of Glentarf; the Glen of the Turret and the Glen of Keenie. Appropriately too, in a mountain parish, four peaks form the boundaries — Mount Keen (3077 ft.) and Boustie Ley (2868 ft.) in the west, and Mount Battock (2555 ft.) and the Hill of Wirran (2220 ft.) in the east.

We are moving out of the land of the gamekeepers too. Folk used to say you could tell a minister by his collar, an executive by his ulcers, and a gamekeeper by his wrists and his farseeing eye. It is a pity he was born in the wrong millenium. He has all the qualities that in earlier times would have marked him out as a tribal chieftain.

But if the towns and cities of Britain are

40

*Snow ploughs
on the
Modlach.*

changing, so is the world he knows. The Land Rover and the Snowcat are replacing the garron, and even the people themselves are not as they used to be. Today, if you searched the glen, you would find it hard to discover one really brilliant bridge team. There were half-a-dozen, only a few years ago. And everyone is getting older. They sit by their firesides, unsociable, with television aerials on their roofs, and vegetate while this modern world goes spinning crazily round them.

Even a gamekeeper finds it hard to keep pace. He still tends to think that the matronly hens round his door make richer soup and tastier meat than a chick with a pill in its neck. He even imagines that a joint, after hanging two weeks in a butcher's cold store, tastes better than the best prime barley beef. And he persistently grows his own vegetables and picks

them out of the earth, when he could so easily get them spotlessly clean, in colourful packs, from the travelling shop at his door.

You might almost say he lives in a world that is past. Watch him on the hills, when he drinks from a stream. He dips his forearm into the running water and keeps it there for a couple of minutes before tasting the water. It is to avoid getting cramp, he says. He really seems to believe it! And the odd thing is that he doesn't get cramp as ordinary mortals do.

Usually he has a faithful labrador at heel. When he is choosing a garron he likes one that is dun-coloured with a black streak down the back. He knows all about grouse, their habits and their ailments, and finds no thrill in shooting them. But give him a rod and a river bank and conditions all in his favour, and Valhalla itself could scarcely compare with his earthly heaven,

41

*The Standing Stones of Colmeallie,
relics of the Early Bronze Age.*

as he battles his wits against some princely salmon. If by the end of the day it has refused all his blandishments, so much the better. There is always something happening to catch his eye — like that field at Waterside, where in the autumn well over a hundred wild pheasants go goose-stepping back and forth, in broad daylight beside the road, gobbling up the deliciously frosted remnants of the potato crop.

He has his likes and a few dislikes among the wild life, and he doesn't like hoodie crows. He remembers the first time he saw one of them swooping down to pick out the eyes of a half-born lamb while the ewe still lay struggling on her back. From sights like that you tend to get the feeling that, if only you could make a great heap of all the addled eggs in the world and inject liquid phosgene into them with a hypodermic syringe, the world would be a better place. But, of course, there never are quite enough addled eggs to go round all the hoodie crows.

If you searched his belongings, you might find that he really has a hypodermic syringe, for use on some neighbour during long winter nights when the snow is deep and the doctor can't get up the glen. But it is time we were moving on.

Farther down, beside a little farmhouse above the road, are the Standing Stones of Colmeallie. They have stood there for thousands of years, probably from about 1500 B.C., and so they could be contemporary with Stonehenge and with the Early Bronze Age man who was buried with his food vessel on Cairn Robie.

Stone circles in bygone days were by no means uncommon in Angus but one after another they were blown to pieces to provide building materials for the farmers on whose land they stood. This one alone remains in the district. There are two concentric circles, the outer one enclosing an area of forty-five by thirty-six feet. It is well worth a visit, though it lost several stones and others were mutilated by a farmer who lived there over a hundred years ago. Towards the end of last century the visitor to Colmeallie could still see some stones, as large as the standing ones, built into the neighbouring dyke, and one huge stone formed the central pillar of a cart-shed. The shed and its pillar both disappeared many years ago. But one stone, six feet long, still survives in the dyke.

Now we are approaching the farm of Auchmull. When Sir David Lindsay, the laird of the glen, had almost completed his magnificent castle at Edzell, he built a much smaller one here in 1601 as a home for his son and daughter-in-law. Long ago it fell into ruins and all that remain are a small part of the foundations and one sculptured stone. The stone, now at Edzell Castle, bears the arms of young Edzell and his wife Margaret Wishart, daughter of the Laird of Pitarrow. It is inscribed: "D.L.: M.W., 1601."

About a mile and a half farther on, where the woods begin, it is best to leave the road at a lay-by, and follow a path down to the river bank, for here are the most dramatic of all the varied river scenes in the glen. In a magnificent three-mile stretch of river cliffs and tumbling waters, you can follow the course of the North Esk as it carves its dizzy route out of the Highlands and through the contorted rocks of the Highland Boundary Fault, past the salmon loups and the gaunt Rocks of Solitude to the Gannochy Bridge on the Edzell-Fettercairn road.

On both sides of the bridge the view is spectacular. And the bridge itself had an ingenious origin. A bachelor farmer, James Black, who lived nearby in the early 18th century, was known to be as superstitious as he was wealthy. There was no bridge then and several people had lost their lives trying to cross the ravine. So his friends arranged that on three successive nights he was visited by the "ghost" of one of the dead, who begged him to build a bridge. By the third night he could resist the plea no longer. He not only paid for the bridge but built the parapet with his own hands. It has been widened since then, but it is still essentially the bridge he erected in 1732. Farmer Black lies at rest beneath a finely carved table stone in front of the door of a ruined church, a few miles away in Glen Lethnot.

From the Gannochy Bridge a picturesque path leads along the river bank to Edzell, and for a short part of the way the ravine and the turbulence continue. But soon the North Esk moves out serene into the open plain and onward to the sea.

The Rocks of Solitude

*Even for a future Queen
dressing up can be fun*

(Lady Elizabeth Bowes-Lyon — now the Queen Mother —
with her brother David at Glamis Castle in 1909).

Castle
of the
Secret
Room

King Duncan's Hall

THERE ARE scores of old castles in Angus and the Mearns, and some are handsome and many historic, but none compares with Glamis, the childhood home of the Queen Mother, a fairy-tale castle with picturesque turrets and strange tales of long ago. Its name has been known to every schoolboy through the centuries — ever since Shakespeare decided to write a tragedy about Macbeth. You remember the opening Act, when this Thane of Glamis welcomed King Duncan as his guest. And that same night, in the murky darkness, he stole past the drugged guards to plunge a dagger deep into the heart of the king. A little water, said Lady Macbeth, would cleanse them of the deed. And so the Thane of Glamis became King of Scotland.

Shakespeare's tragedy comes to life at Glamis Castle, for you can still follow in the footsteps of Macbeth, as he steals out from the main hall and along a short dark passage, to murder his royal guest. The passage leads through the thick red sandstone wall into a bare unfurnished room that is known to this day as King Duncan's Hall.

Macbeth was not the only regicide to darken the name of Glamis. Only a few years earlier, in 1084, King Malcolm II died there and early writers say that he also was murdered. You can see his room too in the castle. And underneath the floorboards, on the old stone floor, there is said to be a great stain of blood. But no one can say exactly how the stain got there. Duncan and Malcolm were both dead centuries before the present castle began to take shape.

There is no evidence when the first castle was built at Glamis but tradition says it was in the days when the little folk still lived in Angus. The original intention was to build the castle almost a mile and a half to the south of the present one, on the other side of the village, on top of Hunter's Hill. They actually began to build there. But it was an exasperating business. Each morning, when the workmen climbed the six hundred feet to the top of the hill, they found that during the night some person or persons unknown had pulled down all they had built the previous day. And in those days everyone knew that only the little folk did things like that. Eventually, not content with deeds alone, the supernatural manikins resorted to words as well. A ghostly voice echoed around the hilltop —

> Build the castle in a bog,
> Where 'twill neither shak nor shog.

So the site was changed to the present one.

But that was not the only odd thing about Glamis. The castle today with its many windows and loopholes recalls another strange tale that the country folk have been repeating for centuries — that if you count all the windows from the outside and then from the inside, you will find that the numbers do not agree — because of the secret room.

It was common enough in the olden days to have secret chambers in castles, but this was assuredly the most secret of them all. Never more than three people — the Earl, his heir and one single confidant — were said to know at any one time exactly where it was. And this, through the ages, has been not merely an ordinary secret room where his lordship could hide when danger threatened. Only the most fearless of men would take refuge there, for the devil has been in that room and the ghost of one of the most dreaded figures in Scotland's history visits it every year.

Nine miles north-east of Glamis there stood until two centuries ago the great medieval stronghold of Finavon. Then, one afternoon, all but a single tower came crashing down in ruins, and even that one remaining tower was split as if by a headsman's axe. In the fifteenth century this was the home of the dreaded Earl Beardie, the Tiger Earl of Crawford. His whole

Sir Henry Irving as the Thane of Glamis and Ellen Terry as Lady Macbeth in the murder scene from *Macbeth*. (Lyceum Theatre, London, 1888).

The country folk will tell you quite solemnly that Glamis Castle has an extra window on the outside.

life was tempestuous. As a youth he was steeped in blood, and less than two years before his death he summoned the people of Angus to a full-scale rebellion against the king. But meantime we are concerned with a game of cards.

One day this Tiger Earl rode over to visit his friend Lord Glamis, and they settled down to a game of cards in what is now the secret room in the castle. It was a Saturday and as midnight drew near a servant came in to remind them of the hour—for people who valued their immortal souls did not play cards on Sundays. But the game was reaching an exciting stage, and the Earl and the Baron were in no mood to stop. "We'll finish the game, even if it takes us to the Day of Judgment," they agreed. And then the clock struck twelve and the Deil appeared, to remind them that they would do just that.

Earl Beardie's family records provide no details. They merely state that he "tuk the hot fever and died in the year of God, ane thousand four hundred and fifty-four years, and wes buried with gret triumph in the Greyfriars of Dundee in his forebears' sepulchre". Five years later Lord Glamis died and his funeral took place in Glamis Church, where his tomb can still be seen. But neither rests in peace. Once a year, on the anniversary, the ghost of the Tiger Earl leaves its tomb and comes up from Dundee to join its ghostly companion in that damned unfinished game in the secret room at the castle.

Of course, except for the servants and the country folk and perhaps the lordly Lyons of Strathmore themselves, no one would seriously believe there was a secret room in the castle — unless you went to the laborious trouble of counting all the windows, outside and inside, one by one. Then, you would find, the story of that extra window on the outside is no foolish fable. It is an actual fact. If you go into the crypt, the original hall of the castle, you will see two knights in armour standing on guard, one at each end of an unbroken stretch of wall, many feet thick. It has neither an opening nor any indication that there ever was one. But if you go out into the park and look up at this north wall, you will see a blocked up window where no window should be. That wall is quite thick enough to contain a secret room. And this might be the site of the famous room, though so might a dozen other places in the ancient castle.

It is odd that Lord Glamis should have been chosen by tradition to be Earl Beardie's ghostly companion. The part scarcely suited him, for he died full of honours, a Master of the King's Household and a judge of the supreme court of Scotland. He was the third of the Lyons of Glamis. His grandfather, Sir John, the first of the family, was Secretary and later Chamberlain of King Robert II, and in 1372 he was granted "the thanage of Glammys" by the king. Four

47

*Behind the barrel vaulting, between
the two knights in armour, lies one
of the mysteries of Glamis Castle.*

years later he married the king's daughter, Princess Johanna. When he met a violent death in a feud in 1382 he was not buried at Glamis but in the Tomb of the Kings at Scone. And so was his son, who succeeded him. The grandson — the ghostly card player — was the first to bear the title Lord Glamis, and the first of the Lyons to be buried at Glamis. He built the oldest part of the present castle, with walls up to sixteen feet thick — so thick, in fact, that when the ancient plaster was stripped off, early this century, two stairs of which no one had been aware were found inside.

And now let us turn to the subject of witches. Shakespeare was on sound historical grounds when he brought them into his play. To have them confronting the Thane of Glamis was a piece of dramatic irony that his audiences must have relished, for witches were real in those days and everyone knew that Lord Glamis had not only royal blood but also a witch's blood in his veins. It was proved in the highest court in the land, scarcely seventy years before *Macbeth* was written. And it was one of the most notorious trials of the century, not the kind that would be readily forgotten.

For the beginning of the story we have to go back to 1532, when the widow of the 6th Lord Glamis was accused of poisoning her husband. It seemed so ridiculous to the lairds of Angus that they refused to serve as jurors at her trial. Three weeks later a second jury was summoned from a wider area and they too refused to serve. So the charge was dropped. A few years after that, she married Archibald Campbell, second son of the Earl of Argyll, and then an unsuccessful suitor brought a more serious charge against her. He swore that with her young son, the 7th Lord Glamis, she had plotted to poison or bewitch the king. And James V solemnly agreed that this was so.

In 1537 the baroness and her son were

THE WITCHES' PROPHECY
John Henderson in the title role of Shakespeare's "Macbeth"
Theatre Royal, Haymarket, 1777
(From a mezzotint by Jones after Romney)

D

Two richly carved chairs,
used by James V and his
Queen on state occasions
at Glamis Castle.

brought to trial, found guilty and condemned to death. And before nightfall they were taken up the hill towards Edinburgh Castle, where Archibald Campbell was already imprisoned. Lord Glamis was thrown into a cell. But his mother got only as far as the Castle Hill, where she was burned as an ordinary witch.

It was recorded a century later that anyone less like a witch would have been hard to imagine. She was still in the prime of life, aristocratic and very beautiful, and the watching crowd agreed that she met her death "with a man-like courage". Few people seriously believed that she had been practising witch-craft. It was too well known that she was a Douglas and that the king hated her family. And perhaps there was some truth in what was being openly said — that the king brought her to trial to get her castle.

Glamis Castle became a royal residence and though James V died only five years later, he stayed at Glamis with his court no less than seven times in those five years — in 1538, January and September 1539, the autumn and winter of 1540, the autumn of 1541 and the spring of 1542. The crypt, which was then the main hall, still contains the two carved oak chairs where he sat on state occasions with his Queen, Marie of Lorraine. Many a royal document was signed at Glamis in those days — and some treasures of the Lyon family disappeared then too. During one of his visits twelve massive silver flagons, each seven pounds in weight, were melted down to supply silver for the mint. And the Lyons were so forgiving that they even hung two ancient portraits of James V and his Queen, slightly nibbled by woodworm, it is true, side by side in King Duncan's Hall where you can still see them.

While the chairs and the portraits remind us of the king who seized the castle, there is said to be a reminder also of the Lady Glamis from whom he seized it, upstairs in what is now the Drawing Room and was formerly the Great Hall. By far the grandest room in the castle, this hall was not built until eighty years after the death of James V. It has a magnificent ceiling and fireplace, and it is above the massive fireplace that one must look for the reminder of Lady Glamis. On each side of a great armorial table is a pair of caryatides. They were fashionable in those days and the same craftsman who did those at Glamis in 1620 made similar ones at Muchalls and Craigievar a few years later. But the ones at Glamis, it has been said, are different from the others — dishevelled and distraught — so that every time we look at the leaping flames in the huge fireplace we are

This drawing by R. W. Billings, last century,
supports the story that the caryatides above
the fireplace in the Great Hall are mourning
the death of the "witch" of Glamis.

reminded that the lovely Lady Glamis was burned as a witch. If the idea is slightly ghoulish, we should perhaps remember that people were still being tried and burned for witchcraft when the fireplace was erected.

Certainly in a well-known drawing by R. W. Billings, a century ago, the caryatides do in fact look distraught. But whether his drawing is accurate is another story. Photography gives them a very different look. In the castle museum, however, is a carved wooden figure which might very well be portraying the death agony of a woman condemned for witchcraft.

James V was not the only royal visitor to Glamis in bygone days. His daughter Mary Queen of Scots rested there in 1562 when she was journeying north to crush the Huntly rebellion. The weather could scarcely have been worse — it was "extreme fowle and colde" — but one of her companions recalled that he had never seen her merrier. She longed to be a man, she told him, "to lie all night in the fields, or to walk upon the causeway with a pack or knapschall, a Glasgow buckler and a broadsword".

When she visited Glamis, the castle was little more than an L-shaped keep, four storeys high, with a great gloomy kitchen. She passed the studded oak door and the iron yett inside, and came to a well that had been scooped out of the castle's massive stone wall, when it was being built. And here, still within the thickness of the wall, she climbed the steep, narrow staircase up to the barrel-vaulted crypt, which was then the main hall.

The entire castle looked very different without its present wings and turrets, and the whole purpose of its plan was different too, for it was

King James V, his daughter Mary Queen of Scots and his grandson James VI all climbed this narrow stair at different times. In their day it was the only stair to the hall.

The hollow newel in the great staircase provides an early form of central heating.

aimed much less at comfort than at keeping unwanted visitors out. Though the crypt was dark and cold, it was very safe. One defender at the top of the narrow stair could have halted a regiment.

Queen Mary's son, King James VI, often came to Glamis on hunting expeditions in the nearby Forest of Platir. But his visits ended with his departure for London in 1603. Three years later the transformation of the castle began. A century and a half had passed since the massive keep was built with its loopholes, its narrow stairs and parapet — all strong defences against an enemy. And bloodshed between neighbours had been a normal part of life and death through all those years. But by the beginning of the 17th century it was no longer civilised to shed your neighbour's blood. So the grim fortresses of only a few years earlier became suddenly out-of-date. Besides, those lordly Protestants who had fallen heir to the wealth of the Roman Catholic Church could now afford a little luxury.

It was not easy in those days for a castle-builder to make up his mind whether he should stick to the traditional or go contemporary. At Dunnottar and Edzell the old keep was left to moulder, and a new-style mansion was built alongside. At Glamis, in 1606, the 9th Lord Glamis began to fashion the keep itself into a thing of exciting beauty. That was the year when he was created 1st Earl of Kinghorne.

Nothing was more typical of this new era of peace than the way folk began to redesign their staircases. People no longer expected that a swordsman would ever be needed to guard the stair against invaders. And so there was no sense in having it narrow. The old staircase at Glamis was out of harmony with the times.

To provide something more up-to-date, the wall of the keep was ripped wide open and a staircase tower inserted, with no less than 143 great spiral steps, each formed of a single stone 6 ft. 10 in. wide. It was built in the hollow newel style, with little iron gratings at regular intervals. The heat from a charcoal fire at the foot of the newel came out through the gratings and took the chill off the air. Though it was not the only staircase of this kind in Scotland, they were far from being common.

Next Lord Glamis turned to the roof, with its parapets from which defenders could hurl down defiance and other things on the heads of attackers. Parapets were no longer needed. Gun-ports near ground level were far more effective. But the idea of anyone attacking this castle never occurred to Lord Glamis. If you search the ground floor you will find only one gun-port and it is ornamental, built in a part of the castle which was erected only last century.

Though it was the fashion in his day to leave the lower walls of the keep austere and to lavish the decoration on the upper storeys, there was nothing austere about the doorway at Glamis,

"The quaintest of all
his whimsies"

with its coats-of-arms. But the skyline was riotous. Fairy-tale turrets, two storeys high, soared above what had once been the parapets. There was no room left for traditional crow-stepped gables and these had to be replaced by flat-topped walls. It was fun planning like that. The quaintest of all his whimsies was one particular dormer window, where instead of the usual pediment he built a roundel with a little room in it and one of his beloved conical roofs on top. You can see it to the left of the stair-case tower.

It was this Lord Glamis who built the Great Hall and much of the south-east wing. And another of his improvements in the grand style was a pleasance around the castle. Because of its angled walls it was known as "the Angles" and the name still survives, though the walls unhappily vanished in a misguided improvement two centuries ago.

When he died in 1615 he left a castle vastly different from the one he had inherited. It had been a costly transformation. Even the home farm was mortgaged by that time. But the improvements still went on. In 1620 the 2nd Earl commissioned the magnificent plasterwork ceilings and the ornate fireplace in the Great Hall.

A few years later the country was torn by wars and the family moved to Castle Lyon, now known as Castle Huntly, near Dundee. It was not until 1670 that Glamis was occupied again — by Patrick, Earl of Kinghorne, the future 1st Earl of Strathmore. When he arrived it was practically devoid of furnishings and for the

56

Glamis Castle and
"The Angles", as the
1st Earl of Strathmore
knew them.
(From a painting at the castle)

next eighteen years its restoration became his all-absorbing interest. He added the chapel, with its painted ceiling and walls, painted by De Wet with portraits of the apostles and scenes from the life of Christ. In the inner courtyard he had statues erected of the Stuart kings — and one of the finest sundials in Scotland, fully 21 ft. high. He re-roofed the south-east wing of the castle and, with an eye for symmetry, built a north-west wing to balance it. The wrought-iron knocker that still survives on the studded main door was made for him by the smith of Glamis and the present railing on the roof is a replica of another example of the work of this village craftsman. The original railing was made in 1673.

He planted an avenue of trees from the outer gate to the inner courtyard and these were full-grown when the castle had its next royal visitor, known to his friends as the Old Chevalier and

to his enemies as the Old Pretender. When he arrived in 1716, with the Earl of Mar and a long cavalcade, his first distant glimpse was of a great cluster of turrets, roundels and gilded balustrades, soaring proudly high above the tree-tops. He came to the first gate, where the figure of a satyr stood in a niche on each side of the arch. The gate was thrown open and he rode on with his retinue along an avenue flanked by Scotch firs. He reached the second gate, where there was a life-size statue of a gladiator on top at each side. And there the firs were left behind. It was lime trees now. So he reached the third gate, the gate of the inner court, and when that one clanged behind him too he was safe enough, shut off by three high walls from the outside world. In this inner courtyard he was surrounded by familiar figures — his father James II, his uncle Charles II, his grandfather Charles I and his great-grandfather James VI—the four Stuart

57

The Old Chevalier
must have wondered
what happened to
the watch he left
under his pillow
at Glamis.

kings of Britain, each on his pedestal. The Prince's host, the 16-year-old Earl of Strathmore, had succeeded to the title only a few weeks before, when his brother was killed in the Jacobite army at the battle of Sheriffmuir.

The Prince himself was still under thirty and most people found him difficult to entertain, for he talked little and smiled less. But he approved of Glamis. It was, he said, one of the finest palaces he had ever seen. And certainly he put

Glamis Castle

Glamis Castle during alterations less than two centuries ago.
(From an engraving at the castle)

its resources to the test that night. Eighty-eight beds were needed for the officers and gentlemen in his retinue.

Having dined in the Banqueting Hall he mounted the great staircase where three men could walk abreast, and up a smaller stair beyond, to his bedroom high in the tower. And while he slept the snow fell thick. Next morning he had to postpone his plans to continue his journey. So he slept another night in the little room, with his silver watch under his pillow, and in the morning there was such a bustle to get on his way to join his Jacobite army that he forgot all about the watch. The young Earl was not even aware that it had been left behind. A little chambermaid found it ticking under his pillow, and the temptation was too much for her. Three generations of her family cherished the watch as a family heirloom, before her great-granddaughter at last sent it back to the castle. It can still be seen there.

In 1746 the "Butcher" Duke of Cumberland, on his way to Culloden, arrived at Glamis to sleep in the same bed as the Old Pretender. The castle was still very much the same then, and when Thomas Gray, the poet, came in 1765. But seven years later the tree-lined avenue was

almost completely destroyed in a few hours by a raging hurricane.

Fashions were changing again by that time. "Capability" Brown had decreed that gentlemen's houses should have parkish surrounds and this was a fashion which suited the needs of the day. Every scrap of stone was wanted for the dry-stane dykes which were turning the moorland into fields in an agricultural revolution. The "Angles" at Glamis Castle were tumbled down in the process and only the three gateways were left. They were re-erected at the three entrances to the new park, where they can still be seen.

In the summer of 1793, while the Earl was away from home, the youthful Sir Walter Scott visited the castle and spent a night alone in one of the bedrooms in the tower. He found it an unnerving experience. "I must own," he wrote, "that when I heard door after door shut, after my conductor had retired, I began to consider myself as too far from the living and somewhat too near the dead. We had passed through what is called the King's Room, a vaulted apartment garnished with stags' antlers and other trophies of the chase, and said by tradition to be the spot of Malcolm's murder . . . In spite of the truth of history, the whole night scene in Macbeth's Castle rushed at once upon me."

Scott never forgot that visit to Glamis. The castle is said to have been his model for Glenallan House in *The Antiquary*. And many years later he recorded his thoughts on the removal of "The Angles": "It is thirty years and upwards since I have seen Glammis, but I have not yet forgotten or forgiven the atrocity which, under pretence of improvement, deprived that lordly place of its appropriate accompaniments, 'leaving an ancient dome and towers like these, beggared and outraged'."

Although Glamis Castle has been famous through the centuries, a new and still more notable chapter opened with the wedding in Westminster Abbey, in 1923, of Lady Elizabeth Bowes-Lyon and the Duke of York. Sixteen years later he succeeded his brother as King George VI and this daughter of Glamis became Queen. Princess Margaret was born there and many a time the Royal Standard has been flying over the castle.

Thus it acquired its royal apartments. Visitors today can see the Queen Mother's bedroom and sitting-room. On the four-poster bed is a patchwork bedspread, made by her mother, Cecilia Countess of Strathmore, and her work can also be seen on the canopy, round the inside of which she lovingly embroidered the names of all her children.

The Royal Apartments are in one of the oldest parts of the castle, in the south-east wing, close to the staircase tower. As soon as you enter the sitting room your eye is caught by a little seat — a projecting stone slab — just inside the door. If you go there when the crowds have departed and everything is quiet, and if you keep very still and silent, just watching, you may get a very special thrill by suddenly finding there is a little page boy, in doublet and hose, perched on the seat. You have to beware of that mischievous imp. He has a twinkle in his eye and a habit of putting out his foot to trip the unwary. It is bad enough having a step just inside the door, without also having a page boy to add to the hazards. Many a person has stumbled there. But Glamis is a castle where

THE QUEEN MOTHER'S BEDROOM
Round the inside of the canopy of the four-poster bed, the Countess of Strathmore embroidered the names of her ten children.

*There is a seat for a very special page boy
just inside the door of the Tapestry Room,
the Queen Mother's sitting room, at
Glamis.*

the ghosts of the past are all around you.

When you leave the castle don't go hurrying off. There is something else that is special in the village — the famous Angus Folk Museum. For older people, from town or country, this is a wonderful place for reviving memories of things that once were very familiar. For younger people it is a revelation of Scottish life and crafts at a time when people had still not felt the impact of this age of mass-production.

The flowery road
to the hills of Clova.

Land
of the
Wild
Flowers

FIVE MILES north of Kirriemuir lies Cortachy, where Glen Clova and Glen Prosen meet. On top of a hill overlooking the scene is the Airlie monument and from it you can see in a wide sweep far up the glens to the encircling mountains beyond, and along the braes of Angus and across the lowlands where the South Esk meanders towards the distant sea. You are in the land of the Ogilvys of Airlie. You are also in a land where very obviously the far-distant Ice Age has left its mark. And botanists all over Britain know it for the richness of its plant life. You don't need a garden if you live in Glen Clova. From end to end its roadside is carpeted with great clusters of wild flowers.

Down in a hollow at the foot of the glen is Cortachy Castle, nestling in a wooded amphitheatre beside the South Esk. Few places have a lovelier setting than this home of the Earl of Airlie.

The oldest part is the circular tower, with a rectangular room corbelled out on top. It is believed to have been built by a laird of Clova early in the sixteenth century, but there was a laird's house at Cortachy long before then. Hundreds of years earlier the barony belonged to the Earls of Strathern and one charter still preserved in the charter room gives proof of a manor house at Cortachy as early as 1330. The barony passed later to the Douglas family and in 1473 it came into the hands of Thomas Ogilvy of Clova. In 1625 the laird of Clova

63

Cortachy
Castle

transferred it to the head of his family, James Lord Ogilvy, who was later to become the first Earl of Airlie.

Cortachy Castle has remained with the family ever since and has been their principal seat for many a year. Although it was not built to withstand a siege — even the walls of the old tower are not specially thick — it has seen stirring times, for the Ogilvys of Airlie through the ages have been the faithful champions of many a glorious lost cause. There is probably not another family in Scotland that so long and consistently ignored the heavy cost of the loyalty it gave to the Stuart kings.

The first Earl helped Charles I against the Covenanters, so the Duke of Argyll came with an army and burned two of his houses in Glenisla — Forter Castle and Airlie, "the bonnie house of Airlie". The heroism of the Earl's daughter-in-law, Lady Ogilvy, when Argyll arrived with his army, is commemorated in one of the most famous of Scottish ballads.

There was another example of the courage of the Airlie womenfolk only a few years later. Lord Ogilvy was taken prisoner while fighting for the king, and was sent to prison in St Andrews Castle to await his death. There he was visited by his sister on the night before his execution and he escaped in her clothes, while she stayed on to face his warders when they opened the door next morning.

Five years later, with Charles I beheaded, the youthful Charles II arrived in Perth as a virtual prisoner of the Covenanters. He ran away and, hoping to rally the Highland chiefs to his side, came to Cortachy Castle only to find that the Earl was not at home. The room where he slept is still known as the "King's Bedroom" and two books which he left behind — a Prayer Book and a volume of Euclid — are still treasured

64

possessions of the Airlie family. But the Highlanders failed to rally to his side. He spent the next night unhappily on a bed of rushes in a humble cottage in Glen Clova, and there the Covenanters found him the following day. Almost gladly he went back with them to Perth.

Most of the present castle was built in the next sixty years by the third Earl, one of the few Earls of Airlie who were blessed with a peaceful life. But though he was too old to play an active part in the Jacobite Rising of 1715, his eldest son joined the Jacobite army and spent eight years in exile afterwards.

In 1745 the next Earl stayed discreetly at home, to safeguard the estate if all went wrong again. But, with his blessing, the 25-year-old Lord Ogilvy led 600 men of Angus and the Mearns into England and back to the field of Culloden, in the army of Bonnie Prince Charlie. And, like several other Jacobite ladies of quality, Lady Ogilvy went too. Her husband escaped by way of Norway to France but she was less fortunate. Taken prisoner at Culloden, she spent three months in Edinburgh Castle, and then with the aid of her sister, who was also a prisoner, she vanished from the castle one day and got over the sea to rejoin her husband in France. On the way she had one

very awkward moment, when at Hull she was arrested on suspicion of being Bonnie Prince Charlie in disguise. About ten years later she died in exile. Her husband had to stay a further twenty years before he was pardoned and allowed to return to Cortachy.

Among the heirlooms preserved in the castle is an ancient drum that is part of the legend of the Airlie family. According to an old tradition, when Airlie Castle was burnt by the Earl of Argyll, a Cameron drummer died in the flames. And ever since then the muffled beat of a drum is said to sound when an Earl of Airlie is dying. Several people during the past century have sworn that they heard the death beat.

On the hillside above the castle is the hamlet of Dykehead and, just beyond, the road branches in two, the left-hand fork leading into Glen Prosen, while the other continues up Glen Clova. On Tulloch Hill between the glens stands the Airlie monument. It was erected in memory of the 10th Earl of Airlie, the present Earl's grandfather, who was killed in action in the Boer War.

You have to go far up the glen, however, to find the loveliest part of Clova, around the Milton and beyond. In the grounds of the hotel at the Milton you can still see the old meal mill,

The old tower, Cortachy Castle.

*The Airlie
Monument*

with its water wheel, which gave the hamlet its name. And in a hollow beside the school, if you search among the rushes and moss, you will discover a little stone font inscribed along the front: "Arabella Marie Ogilvy of Glen Clova." This is the neglected memorial to an almost forgotten poet who wrote *Willie Wabster's Wooing and Wedding on the Grampian Mountains*. Published in 1868, it told of a drouthy glensman who was chased through peat bogs and over the moor, by a witch who wanted to marry him and a minister hell-bent on performing the ceremony.

Even when Arabella Ogilvy was alive the glen was a lonely place. But there were memories then of very different times, before the lairds combined to turn the hills into one great deer forest, stretching as far as Balmoral. The story of Willie Wabster's Wooing is told by an old

granny, sitting at her fireside, and at one part she sadly contrasts the emptiness of the 1860s with the bustling scenes of her childhood, before the crofters were driven from their cottages:

> "The biggins were as throng as divots,
>   Or sparks in ony swiddie's skivets.
> Waes me! the biggins I hae seen
> Are maist dung doon, or far atween —
> On ilk cauld hearthstane the moss graws green,
> On broken beild and crumbling heap
> The bracken waves, the lichens creep —
>   The families gaed far awa
>   Till Ireland and America."

A trail of empty cottages was left in many parts of the Highlands in those days.

The handsome church at the Milton never saw the busy times in the glen. It was not built until 1855. But there was an older one on the same site, with jougs outside for punishing the more wayward of the glensfolk. Even those

Glen Clova from the Viewpoint

jougs were not punishment enough for one parishioner. On a Sunday in 1662 there was no service at Cortachy, because the minister was up at the Milton attending "the executione of Margaret Adamson who was burnt there for ane witch".

Much more interesting than the history of Glen Clova, however, are its mountain slopes and the plants which grow there. It displays all the evidence that it was carved by an Ice Age glacier. For mile after mile the broad valley runs flat between precipitous hills, and down at the foot of the glen are the moraines that the glacier left behind. High on the hillsides too you can see the corries that were scooped out by hanging glaciers more than ten thousand years ago. You get the feeling that if, like so many other things in this modern world, glaciers could be produced on the assembly line, you would be bound to find a standard size that would fit neatly into this glen. And then it would look just as it did in the Ice Age. But Clova's plants of today are more exciting than its glaciers of long ago. The only mountain in Britain more widely famous for its alpine flora is Ben Lawers overlooking Loch Tay.

It was upwards of two centuries ago that the wealth of rare plants in Clova was discovered by George Don, a Forfar man who enriched science and made himself bankrupt by his love of the plants around him. Among a host of rarities he found three that had until then been thought to grow nowhere in Britain, and two others were completely unknown even as foreign plants to the botanists of his day.

He made his rarest finds in almost inaccessible places, high among the hills, but it was not by accident that he found them there. Even at the foot of the glen, on the edge of the Lowlands, there were flowers that were little known. And all along the road to the hills they sign-posted the way to what lay beyond. By the time Don had covered the eleven miles up to the Milton he was in the heart of the flower country.

Even the inn at the Milton is, of course, unusual. It must be the only one in the country where, if you want a little something in your whisky, you can fill your glass to the top with brandy free of charge. That is an old Milton custom. But George Don was more interested in climbing the hill behind the inn. There, at a height of fully 2000 ft. above sea level, in one of those corries sculptured in the Ice Age, he found a gloomy loch almost encircled by precipices. If he had brought a fishing rod, he might have caught a pike in that loch. It is said that an angler was forbidden to fish there and out of spite he brought the pike from Rescobie Loch to eat up the trout. But if the story is true they are taking a long time to finish their banquet. There were pike in Loch Brandy when George Don was there and the trout supply is still not exhausted. Yet the rare plants around the loch are of even more ancient lineage.

It was on the banks of the Corrie Burn, close to this lochan, that Don made some of his finds. He made others beside Loch Wharrel, another hill loch a mile to the south-east of Brandy. High on the hills across the glen, just opposite the inn, you might have seen him joyfully on his hands and knees on the rocky bank of some waterfall near the summit of Carlowie, and higher still on the Bassies and the Scorie, near Braedownie. The native Scottish azalea, the dwarf *A. procumbens*, was among the plants he found there, covering the ground with its splash of crimson flowers. In the corrie of Ben Hard, too, he saw for the first time the alpine *Saxifraga nivalis*. And snow saxifrage was a name which suited it. When you looked at its compact rosette of leaves, you got the feeling that Nature had designed it specially for survival, no matter how fiercely the blizzards might sweep across the high precipices where it made its home.

But it was beyond Braedownie, in Glen Doll and along the cliffs of Glen Fee, that this Forfar naturalist found the rarest of his plants. The blue alpine sow-thistle was one of these, growing on a rock ledge by a waterfall, high on Craig Maid. The yellow oxytropis (*O. campestris*) was another. It was to be seen in one place only, clinging all the way up a narrow vertical strip of rock, and spreading neither to left nor right. It grew nowhere else in the glen. As far as the botanists of his day were aware, you could have searched all the rest of Britain without finding it. Farther on between Glen Doll and the top of Glen Isla he found something no less rare, the mountain sedge *Carex rariflora*, in a peat bog on Little Kilrannoch.

The night he found that sedge he probably pitched his tent among the lonely hills. He often slept out of doors. But other botanists, who followed him to Little Kilrannoch in succeeding years, preferred the shelter of a roof for the night in the nearby shieling of Lunkar,

Entrance to Glen Doll

at the head of Glen Doll. Cattle from the glens no longer grazed at this shieling in the summer months. Sheep had now taken their place and Lunkar had become the summer home of the shepherds. It was the humblest of dwellings, with a thatched roof and only a small square hole for a window. When nights were chilly, they blocked the window opening with a board and a peat fire was lit on the floor. The smoke drifted out through a hole at the end of the roof, when the weather was calm and dry. On stormy nights and wet ones, it lingered inside instead and blackened the walls with its soot. But there was always a welcome for footsore botanists at Lunkar, and a supper of oatmeal with boiling water poured on top and a sprinkling of salt. Sometimes there was even the luxury of butter or milk. The plant-hunters and the shepherds sat round the fire on a sunk, a bench made of turf, to eat their meal and they slept on a heather bed.

Maybe, when the botanists returned from the wilds of Glen Doll to their feather beds at home, they vaguely wondered whether Don had imagined his more startling discoveries. It was hard to keep up with an enthusiast like him. He had records of upwards of ninety local flowering plants, every one of them regarded elsewhere as extremely rare.

There was, for example, the alpine coltsfoot, well known in the Austrian mountains as *Homogyne alpina* but utterly unknown in Britain. In 1813, a year before he died, he claimed that he had just seen it with its kidney-shaped leaves and woolly stem, on rocks by a rivulet in the high mountains of Clova. He even had a specimen to prove it. But the years slipped past and no one else could find any trace of this alpine coltsfoot. So the certainty grew that he was wrong. Someone, obviously, had sent him a cutting from Austria for his garden and he had forgotten where it came from. That was the only logical conclusion — until another botanist rediscovered it in 1951. It covered only a few square feet of ground and it was almost, perhaps exactly, at the spot described by Don over a hundred and fifty years before.

But he was not the only field botanist who made finds that got lost again in Clova. A few years after his death the alpine milk-vetch with its purple clusters was seen by another botanist and half-a-century passed before it was re-discovered where it had been before. So there is still the possibility that other two plants described by Don — the *Potentilla tridentata* and the *Ranunculus alpestris* — will some day come to light there again. The finding of

individual rarities, however, was not his greatest achievement. It was Clova itself that he discovered and he blazed a trail which countless others have followed since.

Yet there were some things that he did not know about the plants on those hills. He was dead thirty years before anyone began to realise that there was something slightly odd about many of the rarest of them. They were more like plants of the Arctic than those you would find on a Swiss mountainside. And that induced a couple of scientists to do a traffic census at the haunts of those Clova rarities, some eighty years ago. They made some remarkable discoveries, while they carefully counted the bees and other insects that visited the flowers. They found that evolution was playing no part in the life of some of those plants. Unable to rely on cross-pollination, they had become self-pollinating and unchangeable. And yet by a miracle they had survived in their present locality, not just for a few years but for ten thousand years and more. They were as old at least as the glacier which once filled the bed of Glen Clova.

It has not been easy, of course, to keep them safe from the collectors. William Gardiner, in his "Flora of Forfarshire" in 1848, described the glen's unique *Carex rariflora*. Few botanists, he wrote, cared to leave the district without a sample of it. That same year the professor of botany at Edinburgh University wrote an article in a learned magazine about an excursion he made with a party of students to Clova. There was something peculiarly attractive about the collecting of alpine plants, he wrote, and at the head of the list of attractions he put their comparative rarity. Then he named the ones of special interest and among these he included the blue sow-thistle, the yellow oxytropis, the red mountain catchfly and the alpine milk-vetch. Very few collectors would have been needed to make those vanish from the British flora. It was not the collectors who saved them for posterity but the fact that often they thrived only on inaccessible ledges. At times, of course, even Nature herself was no help. By far the best place in Britain to see the blue sow-thistle was at one spot in Glen Clova — until a few years ago the plant disappeared in a flood.

Yet some of the rare ones which Don knew so well are still surviving and no less rare today. The yellow oxytropis still grows in Glen Fee. The only other place in Britain where you will see it is in a remote part of the Perthshire Highlands. The red mountain catchfly still grows on Little Kilrannoch. There is only one other place for it as well, in a precipitous gully on

Glen Doll

the Cumberland hills. Loveliest of the lady's mantles is the alpine *Alchemilla conjuncta*, a favourite in gardens up and down the country. In its native state you can see it growing in only two places — far up Glen Clova and in Glen Sannox on the Isle of Arran. *Carex norvegica*, the rarest of the sedges, was not found until after Don's death, but this too is known to grow in only one place outside of the Clova district, in Glen Lyon in Perthshire. The rarest of all those mountain plants is *Homogyne alpina*, which is not known to exist anywhere in Britain except in Clova.

There are others, scarcely less rare than these, like that "sweetest and loveliest of our native flowers", the two-flowered linnaea, which grows in Glen Doll. And any expert will tell you that the very rare horsetail *Equisetum pratense* and that beautiful woolly willow *Salex lanata* nowhere look quite as magnificent as in their stations in Glen Fee. Clova is a district which is special by any standard.

And the scenery on those hills is rather special too. At Braedownie, two famous paths take their separate ways north. One, by Moulzie and the Capel Mounth, reaches Glen Muick at the royal shooting lodge of Allt-na-Guibhsaich. The other, by Glen Doll and Jock's Road, goes over the shoulder of Lochnagar on its way to Glen Callater and Braemar. And oddly enough, when you get on to the high tops you find yourself not among crags and gullies but on a broad moor some 3000 ft. above sea level. Long ago it was very truly pointed out that "there is more level ground on the tops of these mountains than in the valleys below."

But that does not apply to Lochnagar. Nineteen hills in Scotland are higher than it but none more awesome. To the climber it offers an endless challenge with its great crescent of cliffs, towering above the little loch whose name it bears. All around its eastern corrie are spots that bring back memories to the rock climber — the Red Spout, the Black Spout with its Crumbling Cranny, the Giant's Head Chimney, the Sunset Buttress rising like a steeple, the Gargoyle Buttress, the grimly forbidding Eagle's Ridge and many more. But now we have crossed from Angus into Aberdeenshire. Braemar is only eleven miles away.

71

Behind the old manse is the
White Caterthun, a 2500-year-old
hill fort where a witch left her
mark.

Ghaisties
and
Ghoulies

Monument to a Devil-chasing minister

OF ALL the longer glens of Angus, the least familiar to most people is Lethnot. It has been called the anglers' glen and certainly every second person you meet there is likely to be a fisherman. But there is more to be found in this lonely glen than just salmon and trout.

It is strange that Glenesk and Lethnot should be so close together and yet so different in character. There is more life in Glenesk than in any of the other glens and the folk are by nature practical. Lethnot in contrast is one of the loneliest of them all, and none of the others can compare with it in its tales of ghaisties and ghoulies and things that go bump in the night. Even the hillocks high on the skyline of the Wirren are said to be the graves of local suicides. But, whether you believe that or not, the fact still remains that every corner of the glen bristles with its hair-raising tales of the supernatural. There is a Water Kelpie — or there was one — haunting the dark pool beside Craigendowie. The White Lady walks, silent and mysterious, among the trees at the Leuchat. Fairies and a brawny witch have left their mark on the Caterthuns. The Devil himself arrived in a cloud of sulphur smoke at the Lethnot mill one night. And here died one of the last wolves ever to be seen in Scotland.

But the most interesting thing about this lonely glen, with its hill slopes abandoned to the Blackface sheep and the grouse, is the fact that once it very nearly became an arterial road to Deeside. There are two roads up Glen Lethnot today. The modern motor road, the low one, runs on the west side of the river. The old road keeps to the heights on the other side of the stream. Wide enough for a horse and cart, it goes up the hill from Clochie, past the shepherd's house at Dikehead, and on round the Craig of Finnoch, past the last signs of human habitation, the ruined clachan of Finnoch. More than eighty years ago Francis Stewart left the last of those cottages and the village finally fell into ruins. But the road still goes on, wide as ever, heading for nowhere. It ends abruptly on the hillside and only a track which is sometimes difficult to follow continues from there.

This wide part was in fact the beginning of an ambitious carriage road to Deeside, begun 200 years ago on the line of the Whisky Road that we met as it crossed Glenesk. The old highway had another name too. Because the Episcopal parsons of Lochlee used to travel that way to the services in their other church at Lethnot, it was also known as the Priest's Road. But as a drove road it was best known of all. By 1790 the making of whisky for commercial purposes had largely stopped in Glen Lethnot and

between 1825 and 1830 the pony trains from more distant parts ceased coming over the hills. But the cattle still trudged along in their hundreds, heading for the Lowland fairs, and at harvest time throngs of Highland girls came barefoot over the hills, with their shoes and stockings in their hands and their bundles on their backs. Each year they journeyed south with their reaping hooks to cut the Lowland grain, before returning to their own later harvest. The invention of the scythe and reaping machine brought an end to their annual journeys, just as the opening of the auction marts ended the journeys of the drovers. And after that Glen Lethnot was never so busy again.

Until about ten years ago, two bridges side by side used to span the West Water near the post office at Bridgend. The modern one, prefabricated on strictly utility lines in the early years of this century, was put to shame by the graceful arch of its aged neighbour. But gradually the parapet of the old bridge began to break up and great cracks appeared in the arch. Perhaps it didn't help either that a handsome tree

The Clachan of Finnoch

The Auld Brig
which gave
Bridgend
its name.

had grown up from the middle of the bridge. The arch, tree and all, suddenly crashed into the river. But the central stone of the parapet can still be seen. Built into an adjoining wall, it bears in ornate figures the date 1725.

There have been many reasons for building bridges and this one was due to a religious conflict. On one side of the river was the Presbyterian parish of Navar with its battling minister, the Rev. John Row. On the other side was the Episcopalian parish of Lethnot. And when the Presbytery decided to send Mr Row out to convert those infidels of Lethnot, they built him a new church — in Lethnot instead of Navar. Mr Row very sensibly insisted that they must also build him a bridge, as the only way by which his Navar parishioners could get across to their new church.

After special collections in all the churches throughout the diocese, the bridge was built by a Dundee firm for £110. But seven years later the builder was still waiting for the last £24 of his bill and the Presbytery had no money to pay him. He took them to court and won his action, and from their meagre stipends the ministers of the Presbytery reluctantly scratched together a further £10. Then they were allowed to forget the rest and the Rev. Mr Row was able to get on with his task of converting his Episcopalian parishioners.

Life for him was seldom dull, if we can believe all the stories folk concocted about him. Those tales are now part of the legend of the district. And of all his exploits the most famous was the time he routed no less an adversary than the devil himself in the miller's house at Lethnot.

It is a remarkable fact that the scene of this strange story, the humble little mill house, a but-and-ben with an earthen floor, walls of clay and stone, and a roof of grey slate from the quarry nearby, still stands on the bank of the Burn of Drumcairn, where the Priest's Road crosses the burn. One gable end has gone and now there is a wooden wall in its place. A few years ago the slated roof collapsed and a corrugated iron roof replaced that. Even the old doorway was built up and a new one opened on the other side. But in spite of those changes the building still stands. It is a henhouse now and few people look twice at it, though many come to see the Mill of Lethnot close beside it. Much more modern-looking, the mill bears the inscription "IY IS, 1772" on its red sandstone wall.

The old but-and-ben, in Mr Row's day, was the home of Mr Black, the miller of Lethnot, and it was only a few minutes' walk from the manse. Millers in those days were proverbially quarrelsome and this one was no better than the rest. He quarrelled one day with the farmer at Witton, two miles down the glen, and at nightfall he set out to waylay him. Mrs Black

The old
mill house.

was all against it. She pleaded with him, she upbraided him in vain. Having exhausted every argument, reasonable and otherwise, she at last tearfully asked him who would keep her company while he was away. "The devil if he likes," said he. And off he went.

Auld Nick must have been listening. An hour or two later in a cloud of sulphurous smoke he rose out of the earthen floor, in the very room where Mrs Black was sitting. But she was a practical, sensible body, not easily caught off guard. As soon as she smelt the sulphur reek, she pushed her boy out through the window and told him to run for the minister. He was already scampering along the road towards the manse, when she turned to face the devil.

Soon Mr Row was on his way, with a straggle of neighbours behind him. None of them really believed the devil was at the mill house, until drawing near they too got a sniff of the "brimstane smeik".

The minister stopped to think. Then, turning about, he hurried back to the manse, put on his black gown and linen bands, seized his Bible and then swept along once more with flying skirts towards the miller's house. Throwing the door open he strode inside and in a moment it was all over. With a hideous yell the devil returned the way he had come — back through the floor. For many a year afterwards, the dent in the earth was pointed out to curious visitors.

But this first minister of Lethnot and Navar had a very human side too that proved in the end to be the death of him. It is said that on Christmas Eve, 1745, in spite of the dismal prophecies of the glen folk, he insisted on burying a suicide in a corner of the churchyard. Dusk was falling as the burial ended and to the horror of the onlookers he jumped three times over the open grave, to prove how silly old superstitions were. He was sorely tempting Providence — and him well on in his sixties.

The funeral over, he went back to the manse and upstairs to his study. Suddenly there was a movement in the darkening room and a pair of gleaming eyes shone angrily at him. "Fetch a candle and a hay fork fast," he called to his servant lass. She brought them and fled. By the light of the candle he glimpsed a huge black cat and doubtless it passed through his mind that the devil loved to disguise himself in just such a way. It darted out through the open door and in hot pursuit he followed. At the top of the stairs he made a lunge with the fork, lost his balance, crashed through the wooden railing and went hurtling down to the lobby below. His neck was broken.

There is no reference to the manner of his death on the plaque to his memory which can still be seen on the gaunt wall of Lethnot Church. Neither the suicide's burial nor the weird black cat nor even the minister's broken neck is mentioned there, though the "Butcher" Duke of Cumberland, the victor at Culloden, gets an unexpected mention. The minister, it states, died "upon the 24 day of Dec. 1745, while the Nation was disturbed with Civil Wars, but had the pleasure to see his people adhering

The font
was half buried
in nettles, when
it was rediscovered
in 1959.

to their religion and liberties, while many others had join'd those who wanted to overturn both. And soon after, affairs took such a turn as he had foretold both in public and private, the disturbers of our peace being dispers'd by ye Glorious Duke of Cumberland." With a phrase like that on his tombstone, Mr Row could hardly hope to rest in peace in the Jacobite land of Lethnot.

The church is a ruin now. It was stripped of its roof and furnishings several years ago. And oddly enough, though Mr Row lies buried inside it, he never saw this church. His one was pulled down in the early nineteenth century. Before that there was an even earlier church, where someone was buried in a stone coffin in the Middle Ages. The coffin was found when the present church was being built and it was laid against the outside wall where it can still be seen. But Mr Row knew nothing about it.

He would, however, have recognised a font which has twice been lost and found again. Probably he used it in the neighbouring church

at Navar, before it became the font of Lethnot Church in the eighteenth century, and it continued to be used there until that church was replaced. Then a new font was provided and the old one was taken into the manse. It disappeared at a minister's flitting and was lost for years, until towards the end of last century another minister of Lethnot began to search the parish for it. He found it in use as a pig trough at Dikehead — and no one was more surprised than the farmer when he learned what it really was. It had been bought at a roup in the manse.

With a good deal of ceremony, the minister brought it back and laid it in a place of honour outside the church door. But when this church was abandoned and its roof was pulled off, the font was forgotten again. For years it lay, half hidden by nettles and full of stagnant water, close to the door of the ruined church, until in 1959 it was recognised again and taken for safe keeping to Edzell Church.

In the churchyard at Lethnot, near the church door, is a handsome chest tomb, heavily carved

Tombstone of
Farmer Black.

with farming implements and the figure of a sower. It marks the grave of James Black, the farmer who built the Gannochy Bridge after seeing a vision on three successive nights. He was not unaccustomed to the supernatural. It was his brother's wife who met the devil one night in the mill house at Lethnot. And he himself was born there. Not everyone can boast of being born in a house honoured by such a visitor.

A mile up the glen is Craigendowie. Here a farmer used to live who was reputed to have a hoard of money, so the caterans came over the hills to get it. It was midnight when they arrived. They took all the meal and bere out of his mill, loaded them on the farmer's horses, and sent them northward with some of his cattle along the mountain track, while they looked for the money.

The farmer had locked his house door but using one of his trees as a battering ram they burst it open. They searched every corner, except inside the false bottom of one of the drawers, where the money lay hidden. They held the farmer's bare feet over the blazing fire to make him talk. They threw his middle-aged wife on a horse and took her away with them. But still he was silent. By the time they were three miles along the road they were sick of the woman's company and at Stonyford they let her down to walk home unharmed. This "gudewife of Craigendowie" is said to have been Margaret Fyffe, wife of James Molison, who was buried in Navar Churchyard in 1712 at the age of 70.

In the same old neglected burying ground lie the remains of the notorious John Gudefellow. Born without legs, he travelled the countryside on his hands and stumps, ferociously demanding the food and clothes he needed, from the terrified country folk.

Many stories are told of him. One day he arrived at a farmhouse and, with an even more villainous glower than usual, demanded a meal of fried collops. The woman of the house was there alone and she had no collops, no meat of any kind. But with an ingenuity born of despair she gave him his collops, deliciously flavoured with onions and butter. "Aye, lass," grunted Jock, as he washed the last mouthful down, "your collops are teuch but tastie." Her husband was less content when he arrived home and saw the hole in the seat of his buckskin breeches.

It was at Tillyarblet in Navar that John fell ill and died in 1810. The farmer gave him a handsome burial. The digging of his grave cost 1/6 and the whisky 13/-, and a poem was written in his honour by James Bowick of Montrose:

There's he who slid from Perth to Aberdeen
Upon his hands and buttocks, as they say . . .
Who ofttimes scared the children from their play;
But now the fearful wight hath passed into the
    clay.

The Burn of Calletar joins the West Water at Craigendowie and about a mile up this tributary stands the little farm of Westside, where "the King's oldest enemy" lived for many years. Peter Grant by name, he was better known as

78

Mill of Glascorry

Dubrach, which was the name of a farm he had tenanted in his native Braemar in his youth. As a 32-year-old sergeant-major he fought for Bonnie Prince Charlie at Culloden and was captured. He escaped from prison in Carlisle Castle. Eventually with one of his sons he rented this little farm on the Calletar and year after year rolled by.

In the summer of 1820, when he had reached the ripe age of 105, a couple of gentlemen from London met him there and discovered how old he was. He took them into his cottage, thrilled them with his memories of the Forty-Five and, in spite of his age, gave an incredible demonstration of the art of Highland broadsword fighting. On their suggestion, the parish minister drafted a petition to King William IV, with a summary of Dubrach's life and a plea that he should be granted a pension. The signatures on the petition included that of Dubrach himself as "His Majesty's oldest enemy".

The king is said to have been vastly amused and without delay a very handsome pension of a guinea a week was granted. But, despite that, Dubrach still insisted to the end of his days that, if he had been young again and had been needed again, he would have been glad to "fecht Culloden ower agen". At the age of 108 he went on a visit to Brechin, in his knee breeches and red night-cap, to have his portrait painted by the famous Colvin Smith. Then, perhaps feeling that his end was drawing near, he returned to his native Braemar. And there, within a few months, he died in 1824 at the age of 110.

Long after he was gone, his eccentric daughter Annie kept his memory fresh in the glen. On his death she fell heir to his pension and later the laird built her a handsome little cottage beside the schoolhouse. After living on the charity of neighbours, the change was too much for her. Styling herself Lady Anne, she turned her back on her old friends and looked around for better company. "There's naebody but the minister's folk near me that's worth mindin'," she said, "and although it be sair against my wull, I doubt I'll hae to mak' them a kind o' cronies." The house in which she spent the last sixteen years of her life is still known as Dubrach Cottage, though Dubrach himself never lived in this home of his daughter.

And so to our wolf! About five miles up the glen from Bridgend and almost a mile beyond the point where the Priest's Road turns up the Clash of Wirren towards Glenesk, a stream called the Mill Burn comes down from the Black Hill to join the West Water. Here can still be seen the ruined Mill of Glascorry. About 1680 a young servant girl, after a hard day's work at the mill, sat down on a bank to rest on her journey home and fell fast asleep. At daybreak she wakened and found to her horror that a wolf was lying asleep in her lap. Terrified, she still had enough presence of mind to slip out of the dress on which he was lying and, taking to her heels, she fled down the glen road in her petticoats.

The wolf had been in the district for weeks, preying on the hill flocks, and no one had done anything about it. But now the girl's story roused the whole neighbourhood. Every able-bodied man took his arms and hounds for the chase. At the spot where she had met the wolf they found her dress torn in shreds and eventually they made up on their quarry on the West Shank of Wirren. There Robertson, the handsome young laird of Nathro, shot it dead. It was the last time a wolf was ever seen in those parts. And this is a story with a very happy ending, for whom do you think the young laird married!

Scarcely two miles beyond the ruined mill you reach the shooting lodge of Hunthill and the end of the road at Blackhaugh. Here the river changes its name to the Water of Saughs and along its bank a hill path leads on to the remote shieling of Saughs, where the Milton of Clova and the head of Glenesk are both within easy distance.

Beside the Water of Saughs was fought one of the bloodiest little frays in Angus history. It must have been about the same time as the killing of the wolf, for the leader on one side was John Macintosh, who later succeeded his father to the farm of Ledenhendry in Fern; and that was in 1699. On the other side was a gang of thirteen from Upper Deeside. In the year before this Raid of Saughs, Macintosh saved a neighbour's cattle from three of those reivers and it was thought that this larger band came over the hills in the following spring to avenge that affront. Arriving late on a Sunday evening, they were away with the cattle and well up the bleak valley of the Cruick Water before anyone was aware of their coming.

Next morning the ringing of the church bell brought the irate farmers to the churchyard for a council of war. But, not knowing the strength of the enemy and with some risk of being outnumbered or outfought, the older ones agreed it was best to do nothing at all. That was when young Ledenhendry lost his temper. Jumping on a hillock he roared: "Let those who want to catch the cateran follow me." And with eighteen others as bold as himself, he was soon

"She fled down the glen road in her petticoats"

away on the tracks of the reivers.

Up the Cruick Water and round by the Hill of Mondurran they went, but it was not until the following morning that they reached the Water of Saughs. And there they saw the Highlandmen at the river bank, cooking one of the heifers for breakfast.

At first they agreed to settle the matter by single combat between the two leaders, but a stray shot killed a man from Fern and at once the fight became general.

There are several accounts of the raid but the most graphic description of how James Winter turned the tide of battle is given by Alexander Laing, one-time schoolmaster at Stracathro:

> Lang time they faucht in doubtfu' strife,
>   Till Peathaugh, stealthfully,
> Hamstrung McGregor unawares,
>   And drave him on his knee.
> Thus on his knees or on his stumps,
>   He hash'd and smash'd around;
> But Ledenhendry pierc'd him through,
>   And laid him on the ground.

The rest of the caterans fled after that but tradition says they were all overtaken and killed. A nearby hilltop, the Shank of Donald Young, is said to have been named after one of them. When James Winter died, Ledenhendry brought his bagpipes to Cortachy churchyard and played a lament at his funeral. The grave can still be seen, near the south-east corner of the church. It has a table tombstone, appropriately carved in high relief with a sword, buckler and shield, and it bears the inscription:

> J.W. 1732. — This stone was erected by Alexander Winter, tennent in the Doaf [?Doal] in memory of JAMES WINTER, his father's brother, who died on Peathaugh, in the parish of Glenisla, the 3rd January, 1732, aged 72.

> Here lyes James Vinter, who died in Peathaugh,
> Who fought most valointly at ye Water of Saughs,
> Along wt Ledenhendry, who did command ye day —
> They Vanquis the Enemy and made them run away.

F

81

*Musica, one of the sculptured panels on the wall
of the pleasure garden which Sir David Lindsay
built at Edzell Castle in 1604.*

The Garden with a Castle

The schoolmistress kept the rods
on her lap.

SOME TWENTY miles north of Glamis, at Edzell, is one of the most imposing of all the ruined castles of Angus and the Mearns. It has much in common with Glamis. The first of the Lyons of Glamis married a royal princess, a daughter of King Robert II, and the first of the Lindsays of Edzell married her sister. Both castles can list among their memories a visit by Mary Queen of Scots and several by her son James VI. Both were occupied by Cromwell's troops during the 1650s and both became involved in the Jacobite Rising of 1715. There was one notable difference, however. While Glamis has been occupied almost continuously for over five hundred years, many a humble town house in the nearby burghs has been occupied longer than Edzell Castle. But that, of course, is not so very remarkable. In many Scottish castles the time they were fit for habitation was short compared with their centuries in ruins. Edzell Castle, however, has something quite unique, an early 17th century garden so famous that one is inclined to think of it not as a castle with a garden but rather as a garden which offers the visitor a castle as an added attraction.

The most colourful event connected with the lords of Edzell — and it happened before the present castle was built — was an international match, the first amateur international between

Edzell Castle with the motte of the old castle
in the foreground on the left.

Scotland and England. The Scottish inter-
nationalist was Sir David Lindsay. His father
was one of the Crawford-Lindsays, who were
among the noblest families in the land, while
his mother Catherine Stirling was the last of the
Stirlings to own Glenesk. Through her he
became Lord of Glenesk. Three notable events
marked his life. He married Princess Elizabeth,
daughter of King Robert II, and thus all his
descendants had royal blood in their veins. He
was outstandingly loyal to the King, and for his
loyalty he was created Earl of Crawford at a
time when earldoms were few. And thirdly, in
the noblest of the arts of peace, the art of
jousting, he was such a "bonny fechter" that he
received a most signal honour. In 1390 this —

> . . . gud Lyndyssay Schyr Dawy,
> Off Glenesk the lord mychty,

when still only twenty-four, sailed from Dundee
to London, and there he fought the champion
of England, the redoubtable Lord Welles, in
single combat. It was the star attraction in a
great tournament which was graced by the
presence of King Richard II and his Queen.
And it got off to a thrilling start. Both warriors
shivered their spears in the opening run. With

new weapons they charged again and the same
thing happened once more. They charged a
third time, with stronger spears, and this time
the English hero went hurtling to the ground:

> The Lyndyssay thare wyth manffull fors
> Strak qwyte the Wellis fra his hors
> Flatlyngis downe apon the grene, —
> There all his saddille twme* wes sene.

A whisper went round that obviously Sir
David had won by a trick. He had tied himself
to his horse. But when that reached the Scots-
man's ears he galloped across to the King and
jumped to the ground to disprove it. Then
"agayne he lap apon his hors" and resumed the
fray.

In the closing stages they fought on foot with
daggers, until the Lord of Glenesk edged his
weapon into a joint in his opponent's armour
and, with a sudden twist, hurled him defenceless
to the ground. That was the end. King Richard
explained to the victor that by the rules he could
now kill his opponent. But Sir David declined
the offer. The King was so impressed by this
noble gesture that he persuaded him to stay as

* Empty

84

The corbelling reminded passers-by that this was a Lindsay stronghold.

an honoured guest at his court for the next three months.

Eight years later Sir David became the first Earl of Crawford but by that time he was no longer Lord of Glenesk. As head of the family he had moved into the stone-built fortalice of Finavon, a few miles to the south. His younger brother Alexander now lived in Edzell, in less imposing style, for Edzell Castle in those days was still just a wooden tower perched on top of an earthen mound, with a palisade round the summit. The tower disappeared long ago but the mound — the motte — can still be seen, across the road from the old churchyard.

More than a century passed and then, early in the sixteenth century, the old castle was replaced by a new one of stone on a different site, in a sheltered spot a quarter of a mile farther south. Like the wooden one on its earthen mound, this one too was tower-shaped, with cellars on the ground floor, a hall above and bedrooms on the upper floors — very much like the castle which had been erected at Glamis half-a-century earlier. There had been a change in fashion during that half-century, however. People were beginning to like a little ornament. And here we see it in the double row of corbelling under the parapet of the tower. The upper row supported the parapet and the lower row would have added still more support if its corbels had been directly below the others. The chequer effect which the mason provided on the laird's instructions did nothing to strengthen the parapet, though it reminded many a passer-by that this was no ordinary corbelling but the

heraldic fess-chequy of the Crawford-Lindsays.

At one time the castle had an iron yett like the one at Glamis. You can still see where it hung, behind the wooden door, though the yett itself vanished long ago. Inside were two large and gloomy storage cellars, with a very small prison under the main stair that led up to the hall. Above the hall you could look down from the bedrooms on rows of young beech trees, planted on either side of an avenue that stretched from the castle towards the church.

The castle had not lost its new look when it became the home of the Master of Crawford, son of the eighth Earl. That was a sorry day for the people of Glenesk. By force of arms he robbed not only his tenants but his one-time friends as well of their crops and livestock. He even besieged his own father at Finavon and, the second time, held him prisoner for three months. The old Earl, at his wits' end, appealed to the King to disinherit this "Wicked Master". So, in 1531, the Master and his posterity were solemnly excluded from the succession and blotted out as if they had never existed. And thus at last the people of Glenesk were rid of him. But to the end he remained true to type. In 1542 he tried to steal a stoup of wine from a shoemaker in Dundee and the indignant soutar "stickit" him to death.

The castle was still unchanged when Mary Queen of Scots held a Privy Council in the tower in 1562. But eighteen years later, when James VI arrived, it looked very different. By that time a handsome new mansion had just been built on the north side of the cobbled courtyard, with an oak panelled drawing room and parlour, and a kitchen large enough to cope with any royal occasion. You can still see the kitchen fireplace, almost eight yards wide, with a cavernous oven behind. It was in this mansion that the King was entertained by Sir David Lindsay, though probably they did their banqueting in the great hall in the tower.

But not even James VI saw Edzell Castle in its fullest glory. Sir David was in many ways a very remarkable man. A statesman and a traveller, he was caught up in the excitement of the Renaissance and his enthusiasm showed itself in many ways. He planted trees extensively on the bare hillsides of Glenesk. He brought two mining experts from Germany — Fechtenburg and Ziegler were their names — and they scoured the glen from end to end in a search for mineral wealth. Gold, silver and copper, quicksilver, lead and iron ore were discovered. The whole glen became a potential treasure house. The mining continued off and on for more than a century.

Sir David also turned his castle into one of the most handsome mansions in Angus. But if he had been asked what gave him the greatest pride of all, he would almost certainly have chosen the pleasance, on which he lavished so much loving care in 1604. This walled garden, with its stone carvings, its summer house and bath house, is an outstanding example of Renaissance art and there is nothing like it in Scotland.

By that time, however, Sir David's money was running out and not all his mines of silver and lead and iron seemed able to replenish his coffers. Even his beloved pleasance had to remain unfinished. The niches on the east wall probably never contained busts. On the south wall the niches were not completed and on the west wall they were not even begun. When he died in 1610 he left his family not merely in debt but "in extraordinary debt". His successors added to the debt, until within a century they were facing ruin. The last of the Lindsays sold the estate to Lord Panmure, just before the 1715 Rising, and ended his days as an ostler at an inn in the Orkney Islands.

It was only for two centuries that the Lindsays had lived in their stone-built castle and it did not long survive their departure. In 1764 its roof and floors were removed, to help pay the debts of the bankrupt York Buildings Company, and it has been a ruin ever since.

Edzell Castle

The Pleasance Wall

*The Burnes gravestones in
Glenbervie Churchyard.*

Fatherland
of
Robert Burns

IT IS said that for upwards of three hundred years the ancestors of Robert Burns had their little farms around Glenbervie. And though that has never quite been proved, certainly for well over a century they lived in those parts. All over the district — at Bogjorgan, Bralinmuir, Clochnahill, Hawkhill, Elfhill, West Kinmonth, Inches and elsewhere — lived Burneses of the same stock as Scotland's poet.

The quiet churchyard of Glenbervie is dotted with the gravestones of his relatives by blood or marriage, and two are of special interest. Found close together, half buried in the soil, they mark the graves of two brothers who worked their little farms on the Brae of Glenbervie upwards of a hundred years before the poet was born. The elder was William Burnes of Bogjorgan, great-granduncle of the poet, while the younger was James Burnes of Bralinmuir, the poet's great-grandfather.

Their farms, close together on the brae, are above the road which runs from Auchenblae by Mains of Inchbreck and Elfhill to Stonehaven. But no road ran along the foot of the hills when they lived there. Even today's direct road from Glenbervie past the farms of Hawkhill, West Kinmonth and Inches was then little more than a rough track. And when the eighteenth century traveller had covered those bumpy miles from Glenbervie, away up on the hillside where the Grampians began he would catch sight of the two little farms at the back o' beyond, Bogjorgan straight ahead and Bralinmuir to the west. They were fit only for grazing sheep but small farmers in the Mearns were not interested in the fattening of sheep in those days.

The Memorial Cairn by the
roadside at Clochnahill.

Though the farmhouses where the brothers lived have long since vanished, records survive which show how simple Bogjorgan was. An auld clay biggin' with an earthen floor, it consisted of a single room with one door, one window and one "loume" or chimney. This was the smaller of the two farms — sixty acres as against the 150 acres of Bralinmuir — but in all probability the one farmhouse was no more pretentious than the other.

Of the elder brother, William Burnes of Bogjorgan, little need be said. His son and his grandson, both named William, succeeded in turn to Bogjorgan. And a son of the third William, John Burness by name, was the author of *Thrummy Cap*, a popular tale in its day.

The younger brother, James Burnes, first of the Burneses of Bralinmuir and great-grandfather of the poet, was born in 1656. He had five sons and a daughter, and a century and a half after his death he still had descendants at Bralinmuir. The last of them left in 1807.

Robert Burnes, grandfather of the poet, was the eldest son of this James Burnes. Born and brought up at Bralinmuir, he became tenant of the farm of West Kinmonth, close to the hamlet of Glenbervie, and there he married Isabella

Keith, whose father farmed Criggie, some five miles east on the road to Stonehaven. At Kinmonth they had their first two sons, James and Robert. Then, about 1721, they moved to the 60-acre farm of Clochnahill, adjoining Criggie on the windswept Carmont Hill, and William Burnes, father of the poet, was born there later that same year.

To the young William Burnes it must have seemed that the whole district from Clochnahill to Glenbervie and round by the Brae of Glenbervie was inhabited by his relatives. His grandfather and grandmother still lived at Bralinmuir and so did his Uncle William. His Uncle James was at Hawkhill beside Glenbervie and his Uncle George at Elfhill to the north. There were other Burneses, relatives on his father's side, at Bogjorgan and Inches. And when all the connections by marriage — the Falconers, the Brands, the Greigs and the rest — were added to the list, their number must have seemed legion.

As a young man in his early twenties he would have attended the funeral in Glenbervie Churchyard of his grandfather, the farmer of Bralin-

For seventeen years the Burnes stones were encased in cement boxes at Glenbervie.

muir, and many a time he must have seen the gravestone that was erected to the old man's memory. Under the usual death's head it bore the now almost illegible inscription:

MEMENTO MORI

J. B.   17-42   M.F.

Here under lyes the body of James Burnes who was Tenant in Bralinmuir, who died ye 23 of January 1743. Aged 87 years.

Also the body of Margarett Falconer, his spouse, who departed this life the 28th of Dec. 1749, aged 90 years.

Altho' our Bodys worms destroy — Our reins consumed be,
Yet in our flesh and with our eyes — Shall our Redeemer see.

Here is the grave of Thomas Burnes, son to the above, who departed this life June ye 8th, 1734, aged 29 years. Also his lawful and only daughter Margarett, who departed this life March ye 24th 1741, aged 8 years.

It was over a hundred years ago that this stone and the neighbouring one of William Burnes of Bogjorgan were found half buried in the churchyard. And that was too early for science to help in their preservation. In 1885 they were lifted from the ground and fastened side by side to sandstone tables with iron bands and cement. A worse method of preserving them could scarcely have been devised. In less than five years the surface of the stones had begun to flake off. After various attempts to find a magic formula had all failed, in 1951 the stones were totally enclosed in casings of cement, with an inscription on the outside. But that pleased no one. In 1968 they were again put on display with a handsome canopy and iron bars to protect them from the weather and this modern world.

If in Alloway and at Mount Oliphant William Burnes's thoughts went back sometimes to the life he had known around Glenbervie, his memories of Clochnahill at least can scarcely have been happy. His father never had a chance of prospering on that small wind-swept farm and one by one the sons moved off to seek a better living elsewhere. The first to go was his eldest brother James. Then Robert went south and later William too. Their father, in arrears with the rent and in difficulties of various kinds, finally left the farm to spend the rest of his life around Kinneff. He was buried in Dunnottar churchyard where no stone marks his grave.

Ayrshire in those days was a long way from the farms of Glenbervie and Robert Burns had few contacts with his relatives in the north-east. Yet it would be altogether wrong to imagine that there was anything uncouth about this peasant stock from which he sprang. Old James Burnes of Bralinmuir would have had reason to feel proud if he could have looked into the future, to see the honours that would be coming to some of his other descendants.

The first of his grandsons to leave Clochnahill was the poet's uncle James, who settled in Montrose in the 1730s. His written application in 1739 for permission to set up in trade as a wright still exists among the local records. He must have prospered, for eventually he became an elder of the church and a member of the Town Council, at a time when the Council was quite an exclusive body.

He had a son James who gave up teaching to become a lawyer and lived in a house which can still be seen in the Bow Butts. There, on 12th September 1787, he was visited by his

Close relative of
Robert Burns and
himself the father of
a distinguished family,
James Burnes was
Provost of Montrose
from 1818-20 and
from 1824-25.

famous cousin on his journey back from the Highlands. They began to write to each other after that and one of the last letters by Robert, on his death-bed in Dumfries, was to this cousin in Montrose.

James lived to the age of 87, long enough to see the achievements of his own family. His son was twice Provost of Montrose, at a time when it was a town of some consequence, and after he resigned as Provost to become town clerk his portrait in oils was hung in the new-built Council Chambers.

The Provost had a son who spent his active life in the medical profession in India. There he showed a literary bent by writing a book of reminiscences about the Court of Scinde. And his services to humanity were recognised when he was made a knight of the Guelphic Order.

But the most famous of the Provost's sons was the fourth, Alexander, one of the most fearless explorers of his age. For the sheer joy of adventure he braved the perils of a hair-raising journey through darkest Asia. It fired

the imagination of Britain a century and a half ago. Several times, on his return, he had meetings with the Prime Minister to describe the journey in detail and he was also summoned to Brighton for a long audience with the King. He was made an honorary freeman of his native town, wrote a best-seller in three volumes, was lionised by society and received a knighthood, all before he reached the age of thirty.

The adventure with which he thrilled the nation was a death-defying pilgrimage over the mountains westward from Delhi, across the arid wastes where the Tartars roamed, and so to Persia. The mountains and desert were hazard enough but the real danger came from the people he met. British sahibs were not very welcome in that part of the world.

There were a few pleasant interludes, however. During the first stage he took part in a hunting expedition as the special guest of the Maharajah of Lahore, who kept up a style which was quite unknown on the Braes of Glenbervie or in the Bow Butts of Montrose. He

The Burnes house in
Montrose Bow Butts,
which Robert Burns
visited in 1787,
still has the bracket
of the Provost's lamp
above the gate.

lodged young Alec in a tent of scarlet and yellow, carpeted with the finest of Kashmir rugs, and together they rode to the hunt on an elephant — in the Maharajah's golden howdah.

Later on, too, he met some interesting people, like the 35-year-old Sultan of Afghanistan, a real family man who already had about sixty children. And there was the genial Emir of the Tartar city of Bokhara. You would never imagine him being so annoyed that he would personally split one of his high-ranking officers down the middle with an axe.

Lieut. Burnes managed to avoid being axed by the Emir but still many a time he was in danger of death and he kept changing his disguise like a chameleon. At first he rode out as a British officer and then he became Afghan, Uzbek, American and Jewish in turn, until he reached the most dangerous area. By that time he was a Hindu, travelling on a pilgrimage to a Caspian port. He made the pilgrimage in no small discomfort, crouched in a pannier on one side of his camel while his servant occupied the pannier on the other side, and he sat cross-

legged to eat his meals with his fingers.

By that time he was in a land where stealing slaves from Persia was the main occupation. He saw one of the raiding parties — about 350 Tartar horsemen, on their way back from Persia after failing to capture the Prince Royal. But at least they were not empty-handed. They had rounded up 200 camels and at least 115 slaves.

The journey lasted twelve months and Burnes emerged unscathed. But he was less fortunate a few years later. At the age of 36 he was butchered in Kabul in his own garden, at the start of the bloody Afghan rebellion.

The Burnes family is not forgotten in Montrose. One of Sir Alexander's brothers gave the Academy its dux medal. The iron bracket of the Provost's lamp is still above the gateway of the house where he raised his family. There was a time too when you could have seen their gravestone in the Old Churchyard, over towards the south wall and nearly opposite the middle gate. But this stone, like the Burneses, can no longer be seen in Montrose.

The arch, inscribed "Victoria & Albert,
Sept. 1861," makes a stately setting for
a modern road sign.

By the
Cairn o' Mount
to Deeside

FOUR MILES north of Edzell is the neat old-world village of Fettercairn, and here, in a tiny bedroom upstairs in the hotel. Queen Victoria slept one September night in 1861. With Prince Albert and several members of the Balmoral house party she had left Deeside that morning, crossed the shoulder of Mount Keen on a hill pony and driven in a carriage from Invermark down Glenesk. They stayed at the inn incognito as "a wedding party from Aberdeen" and that night they went for a moonlight stroll through the village.

Today a massive archway towers above the houses but the Queen didn't see that. It was not erected until three years later, in memory of her visit. She saw the market cross, however, some distance beyond in the middle of the square. On its shaft was a groove, a standard Scotch ell in length, where on fair days the packmen had their measuring sticks tested. On the back of the shaft was an iron ring to which the jougs could be fastened. People didn't much relish having to stand on the top steps, with the iron collar round their neck, a target for anyone who cared to pelt them. So there was not much wrongdoing on market days.

That night, when the young Queen stopped in front of the cross, no one was in the jougs and no packmen were around. A proclamation had been fastened to the cross and Prince Louis was reading it out to the Queen by the light of the moon, when suddenly the peace was

95

The Market Cross at Fettercairn

shattered by the sound of martial music. The royal party, sure they had been recognised, scurried back to the shelter of the inn. But they had nothing to fear. It was only the local drum and fife band, out for their weekly practice.

Next morning the royal party set off again, by Fettercairn House and the ancient castle of Greencairn, for the Cairn o' Mount and Balmoral.

Many years earlier Sir Walter Scott had paid a visit to Fettercairn House in his youth, to woo the laird's lovely daughter. And he spent most of his time digging away at this old fort of Greencairn. He made some fascinating discoveries. But another wooer, more interested in hearts than spades, won the fair lady. Today Fettercairn House is the home of a cousin of the Queen. On the other side of the road are the grounds of the Fasque estate, where the father of W. E. Gladstone lived. The future Prime Minister spent a considerable time there, though it was not bought until he was in his twenties.

At Boghall, at the foot of Hunter Hill, a side road leads to what little remains of the once famous Kincardine Castle. When Edward I of England came to Scotland in 1296, with 30,000 foot soldiers and 5000 horsemen in armour, this was one of the castles where he stayed on his triumphant tour. It was here that scribes drew up the document by which John Baliol resigned the throne of Scotland. King Edward, on his return journey, took the Stone of Destiny with him to England. Under happier auspices many a Scottish monarch also visited Kincardine Castle — William the Lion, Alexander III, Robert the Bruce, James IV, Mary Queen of Scots and her son James VI. But now only its foundations remain.

There used to be a little village of Kincardine that provided staff for the castle and in 1562 it became the county town of Kincardineshire. But it never quite measured up to what a county town should be. In 1607 the Courts were more conveniently transferred to Stonehaven and today the entire village has disappeared — except for one thing. Like the grin on the face of the Cheshire cat, there is still a market cross, though there is no Kincardine. It was the Kincardine cross that Queen Victoria saw in Fettercairn. Almost two-and-a-half centuries ago it was moved there.

The road to the Clatterin' Brig winds on round Hunter Hill until the Devilly Burn appears on the right. Just across this burn at the foot of Strathfinella Hill is Greencairn, where Sir Walter Scott did his digging. Now fringed by trees, the artificial mound on which the wooden castle stood can still be clearly seen.

This is where Kenneth III is said to have been assassinated in 994 A.D. by Lady Finella, and according to legend she committed the murder in a most ingenious manner, with a wonderful piece of pop art. When the King arrived at the castle she took him into one very special room. And there, in the middle, was a statue of himself, holding in his hand a golden apple studded with precious stones. It was a gift for him, she said. But it was a wicked plot. As soon as he touched the apple he was pierced by a shower of arrows, released mechanically from crossbows hidden round the walls. The details of his dying moment may not be altogether accurate but certainly it was here or hereabouts that Kenneth died. He had killed Finella's son and she murdered him in revenge.

A short distance beyond Greencairn we come to the Clatterin' Brig, where once there was a hamlet with a thriving limekiln. At the roadside close to the bridge the ruins of the kiln can still be seen, though the hamlet has vanished. Its heyday was well over a century ago, when a schoolmaster with a

wooden leg lorded it over his neighbours in a style that was all his own. In addition to his school he ran a public house at the foot of the hill road and in those far from temperate days his inn unfortunately got rather a bad reputation, so the licence was withdrawn. But that did not put a stop to the drinking.

Cock-fighting was another of the dominie's sidelines. He used to arrange an annual cock-fight, with himself as umpire, and people came to see it from all over the countryside. His pupils brought the cocks and he claimed the dead. After the fight, he went with his cronies each year to a favourite spot, a dried-up pool, to end the day with a celebration. There they cleared the pool of its debris, poured in upwards of a dozen bottles of whisky, and, squatting around with their jugs, drank until there was no more left to drink. And then he staggered home with his poultry.

At the Clatterin' Brig a side road branches right, over the hill and down into the small Glen of Drumtochty which provides a little of everything — woods and moorland and a road fringed with the purple of massed ponticum rhododendrons in the early summer. Until recently there

Greencairn

The
Clatterin' Brig
from the old
lime kiln.

was even a couple of fords that your car could go splashing through. But fords can raise problems in winter, when the ice begins to gather, and these have now been replaced by bridges.

Beyond, the road takes you to Auchenblae, a village of character with houses uncommonly sturdy. Sometimes you get the feeling that if they had been less substantial, they would all have slid down to the foot of the hill, for the High Street of Auchenblae is even steeper than that of Brechin.

Once this village was among the leading religious centres of the North-East. The remains of its early medieval church can still be seen, overshadowed by the modern parish church. But it was not only in the Middle Ages that Auchenblae was known far and wide. Until a century ago, less godly folk crowded there in their thousands, in early July, to savour the delights of the Paldy Fair, the biggest of a score of fairs that were annual events in the Mearns. Held on a hill to the north of the village, it lasted for four days. If you wanted a cattle beast, you could spend a whole day finding the one you wanted from a choice of three thousand, and the horses and sheep were scarcely less plentiful. But most folk just went for the fun of it.

Our road today, however, is the one that Queen Victoria took after her night in the inn at Fettercairn — up the Cairn o' Mount and over the hills to Deeside. It is a steep climb up

the Cairn o' Mount. In bygone days you stopped your car halfway up, when the water in the radiator began to boil. And still, for two miles, the downhill traffic is advised to stay in low gear. As you round the hairpin bend that takes you to the summit, there are fences of brushwood on the moorland, flanking the road. They serve no purpose in summer. But in winter gales they help to prevent the pile-up of new-fallen snow on the road. At times like that it is sensible to avoid this hill road. On summer days it is much more inviting. You can see the road dropping steep to the Clatterin' Brig almost eleven hundred feet below and all around are distant landmarks — the Lowland plain with the sea beyond, the Sidlaws backing Dundee, the Ochils farther south. Westward is Meikle Calf Hill with a land of poultry beyond, for in a radius of little more than two miles you have a Hen Hill and no less than three Cock Hills. To the north is Clachnaben, with the high peaks of the Cairngorms enclosing the landscape beyond.

There is a cairn by the roadside here. You are expected to add one more stone to the pile and make a wish, before setting off again across the high moorland towards Deeside. You are on what once was a drovers' road by which cattle from the northern counties came in their thousands to the great markets of the south. There were inns for the drovers along the route. You passed the ruins of one of these at Knowegreens, only a short distance uphill from the Clatterin' Brig.

Long before the cattle trade began, there was

The crest of the road
at the Cairn o' Mount.

another inn on the muir a few miles farther on at Muirailhous. About 350 years ago this was the home of a witch of such high repute that two ladies of quality travelled all the way from Montrose to get a potion from her. It did everything the witch said it would. They gave it to their young nephew, the Laird of Dun, and soon he was dead. The only trouble was that the witch forgot to mention one small detail — that their victim's skin would turn as black as soot. So the two ladies and their brother who nearly became laird had to end their days on the scaffold.

Nowadays you don't need to worry about witches but perhaps you should take care when you have left the muir behind and are at Glendye. Here, over the burn, there is a little stone bridge with a very big hump, an awkward bridge that lies at right-angles to the road. You have to slow down to a crawl when you reach it. And just round the corner, half-hidden from sight, is a Home Guard pillbox of wartime vintage, still waiting to blast you into Kingdom Come.

The road continues through pinewoods and birches down into Deeside. By all ordinary rules, the River Dee ought to be the boundary of Kincardineshire. But it is not. Towards the end of the sixteenth century and early in the following one, while the witch at Muirailhous was concocting her brews, the Burnetts of Leys were equally busy building castles that were a joy to behold. They built a very large and handsome one in Aberdeenshire, at Crathes to the north of the Dee, and a smaller one at Muchalls, near Stonehaven, in the Mearns. A few years later the Scottish Parliament solemnly decided to transfer the lands of Crathes from Aberdeenshire to Kincardineshire, for the good and sufficient reason that the Laird of Leys already had lands and a residence in the Mearns. So even today, more than three centuries later,

Low gear for two miles.

The Cairn o' Mount

about twenty-six square miles of the Mearns still jut unexpectedly into Aberdeenshire, north of the Dee.

The river, of course, is not the natural barrier now that it was in the old days, before it had its bridges. Then you had to cross by ferryboat and the boatmen of Cobleheugh, Blackhall and Boathole of Durris could all tell weird tales of the water-kelpie that lured folk to their death on stormy nights when the river was running in spate. But at Inchmarlo there was no boatman to chill your blood with gruesome stories. There you had to face the monster alone, for you ferried yourself across with a rope that was fastened to a tree on each side of the river.

In 1798, when the bridge at Banchory was being built, the parish was known officially as Banchory-Ternan and unofficially as Upper Banchory. It had a church, a manse, a school for boys and another for young girls. But there was still no village of Banchory. That was founded later by the quiet-spoken postmaster William Shaw and a more flamboyant farmer, John Watson from Braemar. Mr Watson had a reputation for being able to produce a meaning from even the most obdurate of dreams and

partly because of this he was reckoned to be one of the wisest men in the parish. He was among the most persuasive too. He had built himself a house called Watson Place, with plenty of land around it, on what was formerly part of Arbeadie, and about 1808 he began to persuade tradesmen and merchants to settle on his land.

Soon the little village of Banchory was growing fast. Within thirty years it had over fifty houses and feuing land had rocketed in price from a maximum of £1 to as much as £120 per acre. By that time it had a post office, a prison, two schools, a Dissenting chapel and three inns — and a bank within easy reach. And its diversity of trades and professions might make many a modern town envious. The seventy-two families in the village could muster up a surgeon, a constable, a watchmaker, a dancing master, the Dissenting clergyman, a coachman, a carrier, a letter-carrier and a road contractor, a baker, three shopkeepers, three innkeepers, two schoolmistresses, four tailors, four sawyers, four carpenters, four shoemakers, three weavers, two plasterers, two gardeners, thirteen labourers and twenty servants, not to mention the feu proprietor who began it all.

And the fact that they settled there was evidence of their good sense, for Banchory really is a very lovely place.

About two miles east is Crathes Castle, built in the second half of the sixteenth century and finished in 1596. There was never a period in Scottish history when castles were designed with more magnificent taste and Crathes is among the finest of them all. To its original beauty has been added another outstanding feature of later date. Its policies are unequalled on Deeside and its gardens, transformed in recent years, are known to botanists all over the world.

Its yew hedges too are famous, for they have been there since 1702 and are now giants over twelve feet high. In early times, no doubt, they enclosed a bowling green, for bowling greens in the eighteenth century were prestige symbols like the cricket parks and tennis courts of later days. Now, besides being decorative, they help to provide shelter for some of the very rarest of plants.

On a summer's day there is an immaculate air about those ancient hedges. They seem so solid and continuous that it is hard to believe they consist of thousands of separate bushes. But in winter, when the snow lies thick, there is no doubt about that. Often a bush is bowed down to the ground under its burden of snow, only to spring back into place when the thaw comes.

The hedges, of course, are only one of the very special features of those gardens at Crathes Castle. Altogether there are about six gardens, each different from the rest in conception and design. Among them is a rose garden which includes winter flowering shrubs, a fountain garden, a pool garden with a colour scheme of red, yellow and purple, a camel garden, a trough garden. There are rare plants from Chile, India, China, South Africa, California and the Himalayas, and every corner of the world. And just as remarkable as the variety of plants is the exquisite feeling for colour design which is one of the special charms of Crathes.

But even the magnificence of the gardens is overshadowed by the interior of Crathes. The connoisseur may tell you there are other castles more perfect in outward design — that Craigievar has more graceful lines and Glamis has a grandeur that Crathes cannot equal in spite of its ornate corbelling, its crow-stepped gables and

The well-guarded Bridge of Dye.

102

The Camel Garden,
Crathes Castle.

The Yew Hedges,
Crathes Castle.

its brave display of square turrets and roundels, quaint dormers and quainter gargoyles. But it has one unique and very special feature that none of the others can match. Built by the Burnetts of Leys and inhabited by them continuously for four centuries, Crathes still retains to a remarkable degree its original decorations and furnishings.

On the first floor is the vaulted Great Hall. And there, above the fireplace, can be seen the most cherished of all the family treasures, the jewelled ivory Horn of Leys. It is said to have been given, along with the lands of Leys, to Alexander Burnett by King Robert the Bruce in 1323.

Painted walls and ceilings were fashionable when the castle was being built. Part of the original painted plaster can still be seen in the Great Hall. But the best of the decorative painting at Crathes is upstairs in three of the bedrooms, where the tempera paintings on the ceilings are unequalled in Scotland. For good measure one of the three bedrooms, the Green Lady's Room, is reputed to be haunted by a girl in green with an infant in her arms. The skeleton of a child was in fact discovered there

during the past century, while alterations were being made to the fireplace.

On the top floor is another of the unique features of Crathes — the Long Gallery, with its oak-panelled walls and ceiling and its ornate coats-of-arms. This was where the baron held his courts in lofty isolation. A narrow back stair led up from the prison. The castle, with an endowment for its upkeep, was gifted to the National Trust for Scotland in 1952, by the late Sir James and Lady Burnett of Leys. It is one of Scotland's more special treasures.

From Banchory two roads head westwards into the heart of Royal Deeside — to Ballater and Balmoral Castle. The road on the north side of the river is designed for modern traffic in a hurry. The one on the south side lets you savour the peace of the moors and woodlands. You can travel as far as Balmoral Castle by this south road.

Beyond is Braemar, scene of the most famous of Highland Gatherings, where "A hundred pipers an' a' an' a'" would be a very small turnout. From Braemar you can journey on, down over the Devil's Elbow into Glenshee, and so to Blairgowrie and Perth.

The Gold Garden, Crathes.

105

Dunnottar Castle

When the Crown Jewels Vanished

TWO MILES south of Stonehaven is Dunnottar Castle, the scene three centuries ago of smuggling on a very grand scale, when the prize was the Crown Jewels — no less! Nothing quite as exciting as that had ever happened there before, and yet marvellous things were already enlivening the clifftop of Dunnottar almost a thousand years ago.

You can read in the *Roman von Guillaume le Clerk*, written about 1209, how the legendary Fergus of Galloway seized a priceless treasure of this Castiel de Dunostre, its jealously guarded white shield. And there you get a fleeting glimpse of the old wooden castle as the heroic Fergus saw it through his slightly rose-coloured glasses —

> Garda avant si a coisi
> Le palais si enluminé
> Con s'on l'eust tot embrasé . . .
> Parmi la sale s'en va droit,
> Si est entrés en un praiel.*

We hear of the castle again in 1336, when it had fallen into the hands of the English. In March that year Sir Thomas de Roscelyn was ordered by Edward III to go to Norfolk and Suffolk for "three carpenters, three masons and two smiths, of the best and most circumspect available, and also 100 archers, as sturdy and efficient as possible", to be sent at once to

---

* He looked before him and beheld
The residence as brightly lit
As though it had been all on fire . . .
Straight through the hall he strode and out
Into a pleasure garden came.
(R. L. Ritchie: *The Normans in Scotland*, 1954, p. 309).

Sir William Keith built
his tower house on the
very edge of the cliff.

Dunnottar. One of the Admirals was instructed
to provide three vessels to take them north. And
to avoid any possible hitch, next day Sir
Thomas himself was empowered to commandeer
any ships and to press-gang any sailors he
needed, "in all harbours from the mouth of the
Thames north". Dunnottar was still in English
hands when the workmen and archers arrived,
but the Scots got it back before the English
masons had a chance to organise the building
of a stone castle.

We have already seen that a baron of Glamis
in its earliest days married a royal princess, and
so did a Lord of Edzell. Dunnottar had a royal
princess too. Part of the dowry of Princess
Margaret, youngest daughter of King Robert
the Bruce, when she married the Earl of Suther-
land, was "the King's Crag of Dunnottar". Her
husband was given permission to build a fortalice there. But like his predecessors he seems
to have regarded the castle rock as a strong
enough defence. So he too was content with a
wooden castle.

It was about half-a-century later that the
earliest of the existing buildings, the L-shaped
tower house, was built by Sir William Keith.
Probably it is the oldest keep in Angus and the
Mearns. The bold projecting corbels that support the battlements are a sign of its age and the
walls are so thick that inside one of them is a
straight stair leading up to the common hall.
This tower house remained the residence of the
Earls Marischal until after the death of the
fourth of the line in 1581.

By that time the building trade was enjoying

108

In the courtyard is a
well large enough to
serve as a swimming
pool.

a boom. Half the aristocrats in the country seemed determined to build a new castle or modernise an old one. In Angus and the Mearns the new castles included Mains, Claypotts, Balbegno, Muchalls and Crathes. The lord of Glamis chose to modernise instead. He added turrets, a new staircase and a south-east wing to the original tower house. At Edzell, Sir David Lindsay also modernised, with a comfortable mansion in the Scottish style alongside his sixty-year-old keep. At Dunnottar too the 5th Earl Marischal moved into a modern house. But his was different. Only at Caerlaverock Castle in Dumfriesshire would you find anything like it in Scotland, for with thoughts of war far from his mind he went to England for his model. He built himself a palace, with a grand gallery above.

A few years later this palace was enlarged to enclose three sides of a courtyard, with a chapel and a spacious suite of rooms for the Countess. On one side, the windows of the Countess's suite looked out to sea and on the other they overlooked the great quadrangle, where there was a well large enough to serve as a swimming pool. Thirty-one feet in diameter, it had steps leading down that the staff found useful when the water level was low. No one is sure today whether the well was fed by a spring inside or whether the water was piped from outside. But at least we know something about the Earl Marischal's plate, which tradition says was thrown into this well and never retrieved. The only plate in it was one silver spoon and part of another.

The well was not the only unusual feature

of the quadrangle. So too was the chapel at one corner. Except in royal palaces this was the largest private chapel in Scotland. And immediately behind the chapel was the Countess's dressing-room, with an outside stair at the back of the chapel leading up to it.

Maybe her private suite was built close to the chapel with the thought of keeping her mind off earthy things. But we cannot be exactly sure. Someone had also decided that the proper place for the brewhouse was just beneath her windows. And there were times in her life when the more earthy side soared into the ascendancy, for she was young and by no means undesirable, while her husband — though one of the mightiest lords of Scotland — was by that time an old man, tottering towards the grave. It is a well-known fact that wise old men do not marry young brides. She left him on his deathbed in 1623, and went off to enjoy a more satisfying life as mistress first and later wife of the nearby Laird of Thornton. It was one of the bigger scandals of that century. She not only deprived the Earl Marischal of his bedmate. His best bed too was one of the treasures she took with her.

Probably it was in 1645 that another suite for special guests was added at the top of the grand staircase. A fireplace in one of the rooms bears that date. And five years later the castle had a very special guest, when the youthful Charles II came in July 1650, just a year after his father was executed. But this visit was more exploratory than friendly. There were rumours that the Earl Marischal was not too loyal, and the uncrowned king merely halted at the gateway to receive his allegiance before moving on.

A few months later, to the intense annoyance of Oliver Cromwell, the Scots brought out their own Regalia and Charles was crowned King of Scotland. He paid another visit to Dunnottar very soon after and this time he was lavishly welcomed. The room he occupied is still known as "the King's Chamber".

While he was there an English army was already mustering to see that the Regalia joined the Stone of Destiny in London. And that was why, one summer's day in 1651, you might have seen a peasant woman riding north from Stirling with several bulky sacks of wool for the country markets. At a leisurely pace she passed through Perthshire and Angus, visiting various markets

The Countess had her dressing-room just behind the chapel and above the brewhouse.

Though the gun-ports must have struck terror into the heart of any invader, the garrison had their worries too. With the gun-ports in that position, the cannon-balls were going to miss the enemy and hit the castle gateway instead.

but selling nothing. She crossed the South Esk by the old bridge at Brechin and then the North Esk into the Mearns, and when she reached Dunnottar Castle she opened her sacks at last. The crown, sceptre and sword of Scotland passed into the keeping of the Earl Marischal. When she arrived home she removed her peasant disguise and settled down to a more humdrum life as the respected Mrs Drummond, wife of the minister of Moneydie.

The Earl Marischal locked the treasure in an apartment in the castle and one day, taking the key with him, set off for an important meeting at Alyth. There he was captured by some of Cromwell's troopers. For the next nine years he was a prisoner in the Tower of London. But the key did not go with him. Before he was taken south he somehow managed to get it smuggled back to his lieutenant, George Ogilvy of Barras, whom he had left in charge of the castle.

As the English closed in, Ogilvy prepared for the inevitable siege. The castle was well-nigh impregnable and he was well equipped with guns, for he had eighteen brass cannons, eighteen iron ones, great and small, and four huge "murdereris", as well as other weapons. But he was woefully short of manpower. He had

scarcely seventy men. And all those cannons were not much use with only a hundred cannon balls.

Getting food and ammunition for the beleaguered garrison was soon a major problem. By sending boats out under cover of darkness he could survive the winter. But there was no hope of being relieved or of being able to get supplies when winter gave way to spring. With the "Honours" in imminent danger of falling into the hands of the English, the next stage in their adventures began.

It was about this time that the English soldiers first began to notice a fishwife walking along the shore with her creel. Dulse had always been plentiful on the rocks around the castle — it still is — and there was no reason for anyone to feel suspicious when she stopped there to fill her creel with dulse. But they watched her carefully in spite of that.

Next day she came again and the next, until after a time their suspicions were lulled. And then, one day, the crown and sceptre were lowered down the castle rock on its seaward side, safe from any prying English eyes, and she trudged back the way she had come, with them hidden beneath her dulse.

That, anyway, is one version of what

The Honours of Scotland were hidden for years beneath the floor.

happened. Years later the widow of the minister of Kinneff told quite a different story, for she claimed that she herself had smuggled them out. Her version is much more full of high adventure — a frontal attack on the enemy. She said — and she stuck to this story persistently — that one day she arrived at Dunnottar with her maid and persuaded the siege commander to let her pass unhindered through the English lines into the castle. The commander was most helpful. He assisted her to remount at the end of her visit and said not a word about the massive bulge she had suddenly acquired under her apron. He didn't even ask what she intended to do with the two great bundles of lint that her maid was taking home from the castle. It would have been awkward if he had looked inside those bundles and seen the sceptre and sword!

You can take your choice of the two versions but one fact is sure. During the siege the "Honours of Scotland" did vanish from the castle. In the following spring Lieutenant Ogilvy surrendered and his wife tried to persuade the English that she had sent them abroad to the exiled King. But no one believed that. With her husband she spent the next seven months imprisoned in the castle and two years

passed before the English began to admit that perhaps she had in fact been telling the truth.

The castle itself never recovered from the battering it received in those months of siege and the spoilation afterwards. Its silver plate, its tapestries and furniture were all gone, when in 1660 the Earl Marischal returned on the brink of bankruptcy from England. For the next thirty years, though the castle still belonged to him, it was lent to the Government for use as a military depot.

During those years the blackest incident in its history took place. In 1685 the Covenanters were at their most troublesome and the prisons in the west were full to overflowing. It was decided to banish those who would not take an oath of allegiance to James II, and while the arrangements were being made they were sent to prison in Dunnottar Castle. A hundred and eighty-four arrived there on 24th May, to be imprisoned in a barrel-vaulted room and a smaller vault below, and the most harrowing tales have been told of the suffering and torture they endured during the weeks they were there. Most of it was wildly exaggerated. Many of them eventually took the oath of allegiance. The rest — the majority — were ordered in August that year to be shipped to the Quaker colony of East New Jersey.

In 1695 the Earl Marischal regained possession of the castle and lands, and by that time they were in a hopelessly dilapidated state. The end came in 1715, when the 10th Earl joined the Jacobite army. His estates were forfeited. The castle fell into the clutches of the York Buildings Company. And that, as at Edzell, created the final havoc. Within a few months its roofs, floors and interior fittings were sold by public auction. The castle was left a ruin.

And now let us follow the Crown Jewels southward along the coast. Eight miles beyond Dunnottar Castle we leave the main road and turn left towards the little church overlooking the sea at Kinneff. The minister, the Rev. James Grainger, was waiting for their arrival, that autumn day in 1651. He took them into the manse and carefully wrapped them in linen cloths.

In the darkness of the night, his wife and he tiptoed quietly into the church, stealthily raised a paving slab just in front of the pulpit, and hid the crown and sceptre in a hole they dug there. Replacing the slab, they brushed away every trace of what they had done. Then, at the far end of the church, the west end that was reserved for the humbler members of the congregation, they dug another hole, and there they laid the sword of state in its case.

The risk of detection was not yet over. The Regalia needed attention at regular intervals to preserve them from the damp. Once every three months the devoted couple returned by night to dig them up and air them in front of the fire in the manse. Then, having wrapped them in fresh cloths, they stealthily buried them again.

If at the services on Sundays Mr Grainger's eyes occasionally wandered towards two particular spots on the floor, he kept his thoughts to himself. It was very appropriate that a devout Presbyterian minister should be the custodian of the Honours of Scotland. And he didn't know that the Sword and Sceptre were in fact gifts from one of those Popes in Rome.

In 1660, with Cromwell dead and Charles II back on his throne, the Honours were dug up for the last time and handed over to the nation at an impressive ceremony in Edinburgh.

Kinneff Church, of course, has been greatly altered since those days. The west wall is probably the only part of the present building which Mr Grainger knew.

In the Crown Room at Edinburgh Castle.

A Montrose Close

Along the Coast

Life was leisurely at Ferryden,
before the oil men came.

NOW THAT we have reached the coast, let us continue southward along it. We are drawing near to the little royal burgh of Inverbervie, which still possesses its ancient market cross. The story goes that King David II and his Queen were almost shipwrecked off the coast and the villagers gave them a right royal welcome when they came safely ashore. It so touched the King's heart that he made Bervie a royal burgh with trading rights it never had before. On the north side is a headland called Craig David and a nearby rock, The King's Step, is said to be the one on which he landed.

But when you think of Inverbervie you think more of sailing ships and of one in particular, that well-loved clipper, the *Cutty Sark*. For speed as well as beauty she was beyond compare. Twice on the route to Australia she covered more than 2180 miles in six days, an average of over 15 knots and a record that no other sailing ship in the world has ever equalled. She is still setting up records. Each year nearly three hundred thousand people flock to gaze nostalgically on her at Greenwich, where she now lies berthed.

Inverbervie has a very special interest in the *Cutty Sark*, for her designer, Hercules Linton, was born there. In 1969 the burghers marked the centenary of the clipper's launching by erecting a handsome memorial to him, beside

115

In memory of
the designer
of the
"Cutty Sark".

the bridge at the entrance to the burgh. It shows the ship's prow rising out of the water — and her figurehead, Tam o' Shanter's famous witch in her mini shift, clutching the tail of the grey mare Meg. And a noble-looking witch she is! The memorial was unveiled by Sir Francis Chichester, only a stone's throw from the house at 3 Market Street where Linton was born and where he lived in his retirement. In those latter years he spent much of his time polishing the "Bervie agates" that he gathered along the beach. He was only thirty-three when he designed the *Cutty Sark*.

Just beyond Inverbervie we come to Gourdon, one of the more picturesque of the east coast fishing villages. Lobsters are among its specialities and Gourdon's lobsters are exported to many countries. You can see the creels in their dozens at the harbour. Not so prosperous but even more picturesque is Johnshaven, with its brightly painted cottages, its great yawning harbour and its salmon nets sweetening by the shore.

Ruined lime kilns along the coast a little farther south, between Johnshaven and St Cyrus, were built about the middle of the 18th century. That was the time when local landowners were discovering that a sprinkling of

lime on their land could make a fantastic difference to the yield of oats or bere. And there was limestone on their doorstep, with plenty of limestone workers too at Miltonhaven, the largest village in St Cyrus parish. But by the end of the 18th century there was no future in lime-working and no future either in Miltonhaven. A limestone ridge protected its harbour and in the 1790s the quarry owner decided to cut too deep into this. The sea broke through and gobbled up the village.

Today, when you go down the road from the farm of Milton of Mathers, you come to a shingly, lonely beach with scarcely a house in sight. The waves still roll in. But if you want proof that Miltonhaven ever existed you have to go elsewhere, to the upper churchyard at St Cyrus, for example, where an old gravestone tells you —

Hier lyes Dauid Brovn, lavfull son to Dauid Brovn and Effie Vill, indvellers in Miltovnhavien, vho departed this lyf the 6 day of Febrvary 1697, and of his age 12 yiears.

David Brown never saw a lime kiln along that coast. He died about half-a-century before the first of them was built. But in his day Miltonhaven was a burgh of barony and a sea-

116

port, with a weekly market as well as a four-day fair each May and October. It had some line fishing too, though the fishing slumped towards the end of the eighteenth century. The thought of the Press Gang catching you in your little boat and carrying you off as an unwilling recruit for the Navy was enough to make anyone give up the fishing and turn to law-breaking instead. And Miltonhaven was right in the middle of a stretch of smugglers' coastline. But most of the people — and all the incomers who arrived in the second half of the eighteenth century—were lime workers.

The only contemporary account of the death of the village is contained in an article in the *Geological Journal*: "The sea broke through and, in 1795, carried away the whole village in one night, and penetrated 150 yards inland, where it has maintained its ground ever since, the new village having been built farther inland on the new shore."

That was not quite correct. There was no such sudden overwhelming disaster. Three years earlier the villagers knew what to expect, when some of the houses were inundated. A massive wall was built in a vain attempt to save the rest. And the digging for lime went on until the sea moved in. Only the wall, at the northern end, now remains. The new village, a much smaller one, was built not "farther inland on the new shore" but to the south at Tangleha'.

One by one the other quarries along the coast became uneconomic and were closed down, until only the one at East Mathers was left. In 1810 it was still employing fourteen quarriers, six burners, six carters, eight labourers, and six to eight sailors fetching the coal from Fife. It was selling 20,000 bolls of lime a year. But all the surface limestone was finished by 1812 and they had to mine for it from then on, at a cost that increased each year. The annual output had dropped to 1000 bolls before the kilns were fired for the last time in 1836.

On the outskirts of St Cyrus we pass the

The lost burgh of Miltonhaven

salmon station of Nether Woodstone. More than four centuries ago, this was the home of David Straton, a Protestant martyr, and he too was in the salmon business. He had a mind of his own. Instead of giving the local vicar a tenth of the fish he caught, he threw every tenth salmon back into the sea. The vicar, he said, could fish them out for himself. That was how David Straton started on the road to martyrdom.

Nearby are the ruins of the medieval Kaim of Mathers, on an almost inaccessible rock overhanging the sea. One of its owners, five centuries ago, was the ringleader in a conspiracy which shocked the country, though people then were not easily shocked. The Sheriff of Kincardineshire was tipped into a cauldron of boiling water and each of the conspirators supped the brew. Barclay of Mathers needed an inaccessible castle after that.

But the St Cyrus National Nature Reserve, stretching four miles along the coast from Nether Woodstone and the cliff-top village of St Cyrus to the mouth of the River North Esk, is even more unusual than the Kaim. Those who are interested in plant life or uncommon birds probably need no introduction to this area, which owes its uniqueness partly to the fact that all through the centuries the North Esk has been constantly changing its course. A salt marsh, stretching north from the river, shows where it flowed before one such change in 1879. The plant life in the saltings is remarkable. But on the slopes of the nearby cliffs it is even more so. Over 170 different flowering plants have been found on those cliffs and the total number in the whole Reserve is over 300. Many of them are not found anywhere farther north.

The variety of insects on the cliff face is scarcely less unusual. And you will find seals as well as salmon along the coast, while the fulmar and eider duck are among the birds that nest there.

For good measure you can visit the lonely

The Kaim of Mathers

The saltings, one of
the special features
of the St Cyrus
National Nature Reserve.

The saltings were
still part of the bed
of the River North Esk
when this photograph
was taken a century
ago. It shows the river
mouth almost a mile
north of where it is now.

The stile at the
Nether Kirkyard
with Beattie's grave
behind.

little churchyard at the foot of the cliffs. There, in a corner, you will find the grave of George Beattie, lawyer, poet and broken-hearted lover, who shot himself almost at the very spot where he now lies buried. The girl who decided not to marry him was 25 and he was 38. She was an heiress and he was of peasant stock, in an age when such differences were deemed important. She was God-fearing and he was not. But what did that matter? He was dead, with his brains blown out! She deserved no sympathy.

And while she never gave any details of their unhappy romance, he left a graphic account, in his diaries, day by day, almost to the very moment of his gory death. It was like a voice from the grave crying out for vengeance, most scandalously delightful. She had done him a grievous wrong. And, even worse, she married quite a wealthy man soon after and went in her carriage to have tea with lords and ladies. She didn't seem to care what anyone thought or whispered. As long as she was alive, people had to be content with handwritten copies of the diaries but these were treasure-trove. They

became a local best-seller when they were printed after her death.

Crossing the North Esk we move out of the Mearns into Angus and two miles south we come to Montrose. It would be hard to find a lovelier town than this, with the sea on one side and the tidal Basin on the other, and gardens and trees in profusion. Ever since Edward I's annalist recorded in 1296 that Montrose was a "bone ville", visitors have been extolling its beauty. You could easily become nostalgic about its past, for it is a town with a notable history. For many a century its wooden ships sailed to the far corners of the ever-expanding world.

It used to be one of Scotland's premier ports. In the Middle Ages it supplied its imported wines and local salmon for the royal table. In a later age its merchants sent cargoes of salmon to Italy and slaves to America. At one time it was a leading tobacco port, at another the chief grain port of Scotland. For thirty years, in the eighteenth century, not even Leith had as many ships sailing into the Baltic. And there was one

The heart of Montrose is still a market place, as it was in medieval times.

fleet of Montrose ships that seldom saw their home port but shuttled endlessly back and forth, with cargoes of Portuguese salt for the Norwegian herring fleet.

Montrosians, however, have always been more interested in the present and the future than the past. They accept that the ancient closes of Montrose are among the unique features of the town and that the broad High Street, with its many 18th century houses, is probably unequalled in Scotland. But they take pride in the fact that today Montrose is now one of the oil towns of the East Coast. It is also still as pretty as a picture, with a stretch of gardens running almost the length of the town — and a beach which they claim is the finest in the country. They take their golf and fishing seriously. And quite a few are knowledgeable about the feathered birds around them.

It has been said that not another town in Britain has such a variety of birds within a four-mile radius — birds of the cliffs and the mud flats, the dunes and the moorland. In the autumn the wild geese come in their thousands, flying over the rooftops from the Arctic, to feed through the winter months on the farmlands round the Basin. This is one of the great gathering places of the pink-footed geese. There is something strangely reassuring about their plaintive cry. Once, too, the townspeople watched while two eagles sailed high over the town. But that was thirty years ago. The geese come every year.

Southward, on the crest of a hill overlooking the Basin is Upper Dysart, a name that revives memories of the pioneer days of the Royal Flying Corps, when a flight to Montrose from England was a high adventure that lasted for days. The second Flying Training School in Britain — the first in Scotland — was established here two years before the first world war. The R.A.F. High Command in the second world war was studded with Air Vice-Marshals who first came off the ground at Upper Dysart to fly their kites over the rooftops of Montrose. And their memories of those pioneer days were not readily forgotten.

There was, for example, the flight of the original squadron from Farnborough to Montrose. They were to spend the first night at Towcester but only one got there. Some lost their way, others developed engine trouble and one came down close to a mental hospital, where he gladly spent the night. But eventually they were all rounded up and on their way again. They passed Newark, York Racecourse and Newcastle, and in less than a fortnight they were at Edinburgh. They had been instructed not to risk the dangerous crossing of the Firth of Forth but to go round by Stirling instead. One, however, stole a march on the rest by flying straight across and he reached Montrose

121

'Montrose pebbles'
— before and
after polishing.

far ahead of the others.

Upper Dysart brings back memories too of its airfield on top of the hill — a long narrow stubble field with canvas sheds to protect the planes. Every time you took off you offered up a prayer that you would safely pop over the drystane dyke that surrounded the field on all sides. For night flying there was a flarepath — a double row of kerosene tins with a man at each tin to set it alight. And when you flew the Maurice Farman you brushed up your prayers again, for it had a habit of going backward instead of forward, in a losing battle if the wind was strong against it.

It was during those pre-war days at Upper Dysart that a member of the original squadron — a future Air Vice-Marshal — shattered all the previous records for a non-stop long-distance flight. With a petrol tin specially made to fill the passenger seat and an oil can strapped to one of the struts, Lieut. Longcroft set off from Montrose one cold and frosty morning. He had so much petrol left when he reached Farnborough that he flew on to Southampton. The whole journey took only seven hours at what was then the staggering speed of about 75 miles per hour. It was a flight which shook the aeronautical world.

As we move on, the coast is rocky now. Down at the shore is the ancient fishertown of Usan, which supplied its shell-fish for the royal table seven hundred years ago. Its actual name kept changing through the centuries — Owsane, Hulysham and, for many years in the eighteenth century, Ulysseshaven. Now no longer Homeric, only its ruins remain.

Farther south is a realistic Elephant Rock, carved by the sea out of the Old Red Sandstone. It is said that in bygone days the fisherfolk used to bring their infants there to be baptised in a pool of water beneath the arch. On the clifftop above is a little graveyard, a lonely spot in winter storms, when the waves are crashing on the shore below and the wind from the east comes sweeping through the long grass on the graves. It is a dizzy spot at any time and strange things have happened there. Poised on the very edge of the cliff one stone records the strangest of all the happenings in this weird burial ground — the uncanny birth and death of George James Ramsay. He was scarcely twelve years young when he died.

Just round the corner is a little bay with a pebbly beach that has long been known to collectors of semi-precious stones. Two centuries ago an English traveller recorded that "agates of very beautiful kinds are gathered in quantities beneath the cliffs, and sent to the lapidaries in London". In a current American textbook for gemologists you will find another reference to it.

Somewhere in the tiny bay, there is said to be a Blue Hole — a sort of Aladdin's Cave for the collector. You will search in vain for that but certainly there are still some semi-precious stones to be picked up from among the pebbles on the beach — delicately coloured agates, onyx and serpentine, scarlet quartz, jasper, amethysts and cornelians. In Scotland there was no place more rewarding and experts had been known to find a couple of dozen to their liking in a day, until recently the vandals arrived with their gunpowder and the bay will never be quite the same again. If you do go, don't be tempted to try rock climbing while you are at Boddin. Those crumbling cliffs are best left to the sea birds that nest there.

A massive limekiln, that has stood at the southern end of this little bay for well over two centuries, once played a major part in the shaping of Scotland's Agricultural Revolution. When it was built in the 1750s it was fifty years

Above — **A** strange thing happened at this grave, on top of the cliff at the Elephant Rock.

Below — **A** gravestone cannot lie!

In MEMORY of
GEORGE JAMES RAMSAY
Born Novr 24th 1852
Died Decr 17th 1840

The Lime Kiln at Boddin

ahead of its time and, thanks to it, the land for miles around became famed throughout Scotland for its fertility. Those were the days when in all too many cases farmland consisted largely of moor and marshes.

We are now close to Lunan Bay, with its sand dunes and ancient Redcastle standing guard over the mouth of the river. The oldest part of the castle, a stretch of massive curtain wall, was almost certainly built for King William the Lion eight centuries ago, and this curtain may well have been the only stone-built part of the castle in those days. It was quarried from the Upper Old Red Sandstone and this gave it the name of Redcastle from the beginning. In a Latin deed dated 1286 it bears that name — *rubeum castrum.*

Though the tower house is not nearly as old, it too is medieval. Four centuries ago the Dowager Lady Innermeath narrowly escaped being roasted alive in it. She had chosen a young man as her second husband, in the fond belief that he would be a comfort to her in her old

age. But instead, with about a hundred armed men and modern artillery, he besieged the castle and set fire to the tower house with her inside. The Provost of Dundee arrived with an army just in time to save her life.

Latterly the castle was put to more law-abiding uses. Towards the end of the 18th century it became the manse for the minister, and after that a little building was erected among the ruins as a Customs post, for smugglers were rather fond of Lunan Bay. But today the birds are left in peace to nest there.

Lunan recalls the name of Walter Mill, its Roman Catholic priest on the eve of the Reformation. The all-powerful Cardinal Beaton had his holiday home nearby at Ethie Castle and the humble priest and the mighty Cardinal must often have met. But just when the Cardinal was fighting heresy with every weapon he possessed, under his nose this village priest turned heretic and stopped celebrating mass. He was arrested but escaped from prison. As the Reformation drew near he became more

124

*The
tower house,
Redcastle.*

outspoken. At the age of 82 he was again arrested and this time he was imprisoned in the dreaded Bottle Dungeon in St Andrews Castle. A full synod of bishops and clergy condemned him to be burned at the stake in 1558.

The shopkeepers of St Andrews are said to have closed their booths for the day, to prevent any tar barrels or cord from them being used at his burning. So the ropes of the Cardinal's pavilion had to be used instead. And the story goes that the aged priest told the assembled crowd with his dying breath: "As for me, I am fourscore and two years old, and cannot live long by course of nature; but a hundred better shall rise out of the ashes of my bones. I trust in God I shall be the last that shall suffer death in Scotland for this cause." He was in fact the last. Those who suffered persecution in the next few centuries were Catholics, not Protestants.

Witches were unpopular too. For drowning them there is a Witches' Pool in the River

The mouth of the Lunan from Redcastle.

The Deil's Head

Lunan, near the tree-clad Gallowshill.

From the southern end of Lunan Bay all the way to Arbroath, we are back to the rocky coastline — and the winter storms have scooped out a score of caves from the soft red sandstone cliffs — the Dark Cave, the Forbidden Cave, the Stalactite Cave; the Gaylet Pot, which burrows through the rock to open out suddenly in the middle of a field, a hundred yards from the shore. There are all sorts of stories about those caves — of smugglers and hidden treasure and murder. In one of them you may even hear the faint echo of a pibroch, for a piper homeward bound from a wedding at Auchmithie went marching into it, playing his pipes, and was never again seen by mortal eyes. But that was not so very unusual. No piper who was worth his salt could resist marching into a cave. All over the Highlands there are caves where pipers got lost.

It was along the stretch of coast between Lunan and Arbroath that Sir Walter Scott found his setting for the opening scene of *The Antiquary*, where a father and daughter are feared drowned by the rising tide at the base of those red sandstone cliffs. On their way down to the water's edge they had passed through a little fishing village and this village of Mussel Crag — a mere half-dozen cottages — keeps reappearing in the story.

Mussel Crag is Auchmithie and today there are about forty cottages instead of six. But the men no longer go out to the white fishing. Long ago the boats were moved to Arbroath. And yet, more than any other village on the Angus coast Auchmithie retains the atmosphere of an old-world fishing village. Artists and photographers find endless fascination in its picturesque houses that cling to the edge of the steep hillside.

If towns and villages had their own artists laureate, Auchmithie's would undoubtedly be William Bradley Lamond. A fine artist of the Scottish School, he spent all his summers there

126

for more than forty years, and painted it in all its moods and facets. He has left a permanent record of a way of life which is gone, never to return. Many of his paintings are now in the Dundee Art Galleries.

And so we come to Arbroath, a popular modern holiday resort with an ancient history. Its abbey was built about eight hundred years ago by King William the Lion, and he lies buried in front of its high altar. It was in this abbey too that King Robert the Bruce held a meeting of the Scottish Parliament in 1320, to approve the famous Declaration of Scottish Independence. The colourful Arbroath Pageant is based on that.

In the early post-war years the abbey provided the setting for another moment of history. The Stone of Destiny had vanished from Westminster Abbey and for months the police tried in vain to find where it was. Then, one day, it reappeared, wrapped in the blue and white flag of Scotland, beside the high altar in the abbey at Arbroath. It was soon whisked unceremoniously off to London in a fast police car.

Even older than the abbey are some Pictish sculptured stones, carved more than a thousand years ago, that are housed in a little museum beside the church of St Vigeans, once the parish church of Arbroath. We have already come across other Pictish stones at Aberlemno. But St Vigeans Church, high on its mound, is interesting too. It is an impressive building inside as well as outside, and part of it is very old. For about forty years, in the 17th century, the congregation did without Holy Communion, for everyone knew that only by abstaining could they keep their church from coming tumbling down to the foot of the hill. And no one really felt he was being deprived of anything special. Presbyterians were less concerned about Communion then than they are today.

Among the special archaeological features of the Angus countryside are the long narrow underground chambers, with curving stone-built walls, that were made some 1800 years ago. They have been known to archaeologists for centuries and until recently it was thought they were underground dwellings. But that has been disproved. Now it is thought that some were used for cattle and some as storehouses. Whatever their purpose, it was not a success and soon they

Fishermen's cottages, Auchmithie.

127

were abandoned, after all the immense work in building them.

There are two notable examples of those souterrains, farther south, at Ardestie and neighbouring Carlungie, but Arbroath also has one, in its Eastern Cemetery, with several modern corpses inside. The gravedigger admitted afterwards that he thought it odd when he found a stone wall on each side of a grave he was digging. But it was only when the same thing happened again, at another grave nearby, that the mystery of the walls was solved. Now the unoccupied part of the souterrain is open for your inspection. And it is an intriguing thought that, from the rest of it, archaeologists a thousand years hence may find irrefutable proof that souterrains — in Arbroath at least — were not byres or even store-houses but burial chambers for the dead.

Oddly enough, though Arbroath is so rich in history, it took a long time to grow as big as some of the other Angus burghs which it now far outstrips in size. About two centuries ago it was little more than a tenth of its present size, with very little fishing and almost no trade. Its main industry was smuggling and even at that it was not very good. Two things set it on the road to prosperity — the building of a harbour and the growth a few years later of the linen industry. Within half-a-century, from being one of the smaller Angus burghs, it became the largest outside of Dundee.

Now the bulldozers have moved into Arbroath and literally hundreds of its old red sandstone cottages have been swept away in a massive redevelopment, and the day seems near when there will no longer be any narrow streets left, to bulge with holidaymakers in the summer months. But down by the harbour the fisher-houses still survive in this changing Arbroath. Here you are in a different world, where little houses and old superstitions still have their place, and the gulls queue up to roost on the rooftops and the aroma of the smoking shed is all around.

Seven miles south of Arbroath we come to Carnoustie where golf is much more than just a game. It not only possesses one of the best championship courses in Britain. For many a year golf was also the town's chief export industry. More than three hundred of its young people are said to have become professionals, mostly overseas.

Farther along the coast we come to Monifieth

An odd thing happened in this Arbroath cemetery.

*An early 18th century shipmaster
built this house beside the harbour
wall at Arbroath.*

St Vigeans Church

The Ardestie Souterrain had its own drainage system but the drain was not a success. The souterrain still flooded.

with its golf, its sand dunes and a beach with a view of the Fife coast. But let us turn aside to see the souterrains at Ardestie and Carlungie. These were discovered only in recent times and so they have been excavated more carefully than any others. At Ardestie the circular houses of the people who lived there can be seen alongside the souterrain. And looking down on those monuments of the second century A.D. is a much larger and very much older one, the Iron Age fort which covers the top of the Hill of Laws. That hilltop site was occupied for a long time. When the Romans were in Britain some native farmer built himself a broch within the ramparts of the old fort, where he could hide with his family if Roman slave-gatherers came that way. There was another broch at Hurley-Hawkin — at Liff, near Dundee — but very few indeed were built as far south as these.

If you are a golfer, sooner or later you will find yourself on the Caird Park course in Dundee and you cannot play there without discovering that you are close to one of the more interesting castles of Dundee. In the old days the town was surrounded by castles. Dudhope in the west, the most massive of them all, was the home for more than four centuries of the Constable of Dundee. In the east were Broughty and Claypotts, the one on the coast, the other on the hillside behind. And this one, at the golf course, is Mains Castle. Its ruins stand in a picturesque wooded ravine, which is now a popular picnic spot.

Castles, like the houses of today, had their changing fashions. Mains is in one of the mid-16th century styles, with a courtyard enclosed on four sides. The entrance gateway is in a wall which occupies the west side, while buildings enclose the other three sides.

The very unusual feature of Mains Castle is its square tower, rising to a height of no less than fifty feet. It was not always so high. The castle stood on low-lying ground and, as time went on and wars returned, it became an embarrassment that any foe could approach unseen, hidden by the rising ground to the south. So about 1630 the tower was heightened to give a better view of this blind spot. The general effect is as striking as it is rare in Scottish castles.

A crow-stepped gable on the north range raises an interesting question. In the 16th century crow-stepped gables were very common but this one is not ordinary, for each step has a little gable on top. Usually this was a sign that the building was ecclesiastical and built in Roman Catholic times. This one was built after the Reformation but its owner was a staunch Roman Catholic all his life, and maybe he felt that this was one small way of letting the world know how he felt. There are similar gablets at Farnell Castle, near Brechin. Though it was once the home of the Bishops of Brechin, the gablets were not added until after the Reformation by the Roman Catholic 5th Lord Ogilvy.

Claypotts Castle, on the outskirts of Broughty on the main road from Dundee to Arbroath, is so different in style from Mains Castle that it is hard to believe they were built in the same century. Yet they belong to the same decade. Mains was begun about 1562 and Claypotts in 1569. While Mains was built with little thought that some day it might have to be defended, Claypotts was designed like an arsenal, bristling all round with armaments. Very few castles in Scotland flaunt their strength so blatantly.

Claypotts, however, was in every sense "contemporary". Medieval weapons were now obsolete and defenders were no longer pouring molten lead or boiling water down from the battlements on to the heads of the strangers at their door. A blast of gunfire at ground floor level was much more effective. So there is no parapet at Claypotts. A round tower has been built at each end of the tower house instead, with gun-ports to provide cross fire against any attacker. This was not too easy to plan. One staircase tower got into the line of fire and the only way to prevent it being hit was to cut a groove in it. You can see the groove in the photograph. Some gun-ports too got into strange places. One was in the kitchen fireplace. But though the ground floor was planned on strictly warlike lines, upstairs it was different. High above, in a roomy flat, the family had a glorious view across the Tay estuary.

Broughty Castle, down beside the harbour, is more of a battle-scarred veteran than the rest. Built at the end of the 15th century, it was captured by the English half-a-century later and they held it for three years. It acquired other scars as the years went on and when Robert Burns saw it in 1787 it was already a ruin — which may seem odd, for it is certainly no ruin today. But castles have a habit of rising like the phoenix from their ashes. Broughty Castle did that about 1870, when the Army practically rebuilt it for use as a gun battery. Now it forms the very attractive setting for an unusual local museum.

Claypotts Castle was very "contemporary", when it was built in the 1560s, but it was too aggressive in style to be copied by others.

Mains Castle

INDEX

(Illustrations in italic numerals)